SHARKS
of the Pacific Northwest

D1707806

SHARKS

of the Pacific Northwest

Including Oregon, Washington,
British Columbia and Alaska

Alessandro De Maddalena,
Antonella Preti
& Tarik Polansky

Illustrations by Alessandro De Maddalena

Harbour Publishing

Harbour Publishing Co. Ltd.
P.O. Box 219
Madeira Park, BC
V0N 2H0
www.harbourpublishing.com

Text design by Roger Handling, Terra Firma Digital Arts
Additional photo credits: cover, basking shark by Chris Gotschalk; title page, great white shark photo © www.davidfleetham.com; table of contents, leopard shark photo © www. davidfleetham.com.
Printed in Canada

Harbour Publishing acknowledges financial support from the Government of Canada through the Book Publishing Industry Development Program and the Canada Council for the Arts, and from the Province of British Columbia through the British Columbia Arts Council and the Book Publisher's Tax Credit.

BRITISH
COLUMBIA
ARTS COUNCIL
Supported by the Province of British Columbia

THE CANADA COUNCIL | LE CONSEIL DES ARTS
FOR THE ARTS | DU CANADA
SINCE 1957 | DEPUIS 1957

Library and Archives Canada Cataloguing in Publication

De Maddalena, Alessandro, 1970-
    Sharks of the Pacific Northwest : including Oregon, Washington, British Columbia & Alaska / Alessandro De Maddalena, Antonella Preti and Tarik Polansky.

 Includes bibliographical references and index.
 ISBN 978-1-55017-418-2

    1. Sharks—Northwest Coast of North America—Identification. I. Preti, Antonella, 1971- II. Polansky, Tarik, 1977- III. Title.

QL638.9.D44 2007   597.3'17745   C2007-900189-0

This book is dedicated to the memory of R. Aidan Martin, a brilliant scientist, an expert on shark biology, an artist, and most of all a real gentleman.

CONTENTS

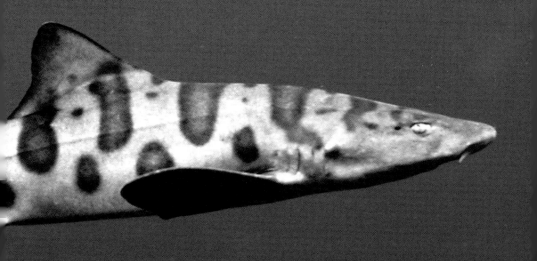

Foreword

Shark populations around the world are being compromised, mostly by overfishing, but habitat loss and now climate change also are exerting their tolls. One area where sharks are generally doing well is the northeast Pacific Ocean, where some shark populations have increased well above historical levels, including salmon sharks and Pacific sleeper sharks. The reason for these high shark populations may be better control of the fishing effort, making the region a refuge for sharks. But to find the answer we need to study these interesting fish, and that's where this book will be most important. *Sharks of the Pacific Northwest* is the best guide to northeast Pacific sharks and includes basic information about shark biology, ecology and behavior that will promote more study. The descriptions of the northeast Pacific sharks is important for professional biologists as well as shark hobbyists and fishermen who fish the waters of this region. You won't want to be without this book in your boat or home the next time you are lucky enough to encounter a shark in the Pacific Northwest.

Among the most interesting of animals are the sharks, and most

Sea stack on the north side of Haystack Rock at Cannon Beach, Oregon. Large sharks occasionally come close inshore, more often in zones where the bottom drops off very rapidly and prey are abundant. *Photo by Carol Baldwin, NOAA OMAO / courtesy of NOAA Photo Library.*

people share this fascination for what is also one of the most secretive and misunderstood groups of animals. This book will uncover the mystery of the shark by revealing many of its secrets, such as the association of its body shape or size and shape of its teeth with its niche or the way it makes a living. An adult great white shark has teeth designed to take large prey or tear chunks of tissue from a dead floating whale, while the salmon shark is short and very fast and equipped with short, pointed teeth better suited for securing smaller fish such as herring or salmon. In this comprehensive book of sharks of the northeast Pacific Ocean you will learn about many species of sharks, some of which are rarely seen even by shark researchers.

Did you know that sharks need to swim or they will sink? But some sharks, such as the Pacific angelshark, prefer to live on the bottom (the benthos), where they may bury themselves in the sand and mud to ambush unsuspecting prey. You will also learn about the piked dogfish, which grows a long, sharp spine on its back behind the dorsal fin to protect itself from predators, including other sharks.

As you read this informative book you will begin to realize that sharks seem to have figured out many strategies for finding and capturing prey, securing mates and avoiding predation. That's because sharks are among the most successful of all groups of animals, and their kind have been in the Earth's oceans hundreds of millions of years longer than the first hominids on land.

My research in Alaska has included many species of predators such as orcas, bald eagles, bears and wolves. But my work with salmon sharks, Pacific sleeper sharks and great white sharks has revealed far more to me about the diversity of predators and the adaptations that sharks have embraced to find food, avoid predation and reproduce. *Sharks of the Pacific Northwest* reveals these secrets and more on all 18 shark species known to occur in the northeast Pacific.

You will learn about the strange sharks that spend much of their lives in crushing deep waters, such as the bluntnose sixgill shark, broadnose sevengill shark and Pacific sleeper shark. This book will tell you that the piked dogfish is common fare on many tables, but it doesn't reproduce until it is in its twenties and it can live to be over 100 years old, important information for species management. The unique hunting technique of the common thresher shark is also described; it uses its tail to stun its prey. Among the impressive facts you will find in this book is that the second-largest of all fishes, the

basking shark, eats some of the smallest prey, while the great white shark can attack large marine mammals, and salmon sharks and shortfin mako sharks are two of the fastest fish in the ocean.

Six of the strangest sharks to occur in any ocean are inhabitants of the northeast Pacific: prickly shark, brown catshark, longnose catshark, filetail catshark, tope shark or soupfin shark, and brown smoothhound. You have to read this book just to find out how the Pacific sleeper shark is able to hunt at night when its eyes have been blinded by parasites covering its corneas.

Over the years Alessandro De Maddalena has presented us with his research results about great white sharks and other interesting shark species. De Maddalena is a seasoned shark researcher, the curator of the Italian Great White Shark Data Bank, president of the Italian Ichthyological Society and a founding member of the Mediterranean Shark Research Group. He is also the author of six other books about sharks. Antonella Preti is a marine ecologist who is working on a feeding study of the shortfin mako, blue and common thresher sharks. Tarik Polansky has a degree in Visual Arts (Media) from the University of California, San Diego, and brings a more artistic approach to the team. Together they build on their previous research and educational experiences by presenting comprehensive lessons about shark biology, ecology and behavior.

Bruce Wright

Science Director, Aleut International Association

Executive Director, Conservation Science Institute, www.conservationinstitute.org

Science Advisor, Aleutian Pribilof Islands Association, www.apiai.org

I know Alessandro De Maddalena from his research on sharks of the Mediterranean Sea, and especially his papers on the great white shark (*Carcharodon carcharias*). So I was pleasantly surprised to see his book on the sharks of the Pacific Northwest with Antonella Preti and Tarik Polansky. I was also surprised to learn that there are 18 species of sharks in the cool waters of the northeast Pacific ocean, from the 27-inch brown catshark to the 39-foot basking shark. This book provides for the identification of these 18 shark species, with spectacular photographs and accurate paintings and drawings, along with summaries of shark classification, morphology, distribution, habitat, diet, reproduction and behavior. It also includes a concise general account of shark evolution, anatomy and physiology, as well as discussion of attacks on humans and details of shark fisheries. The authors have combined a genuine admiration for these predators with the research biologist's eye for accurate detail. An extensive, up-to-date listing of references is provided. *Sharks of the Pacific Northwest* will be a welcome addition to any naturalist's library.

John E. Randall

Senior Ichthyologist, Bernice P. Bishop Museum, Honolulu, Hawaii

Preface

There are not many creatures on this planet that are as feared and misunderstood as sharks. Having always been fascinated by these wonderful fishes, it has become our mission to help extend the knowledge that is necessary in understanding, admiring and protecting them. The aim of this book is to both provide accurate scientific information on sharks and profile those that inhabit the waters of the Pacific Northwest—an area that has a rich variety of 18 species. This volume has been written for those interested in learning more on sharks and is primarily aimed at a broad and non-technical readership. Its up-to-date and detailed scientific contents, however, make it a useful tool for biologists and zoologists. The book is fully illustrated by Alessandro De Maddalena, who has spent almost thirty years of his life depicting sharks. Beautiful photos that have been shot mainly in the northeastern Pacific Ocean by a number of professional photographers, researchers and sport fishermen are also provided. We hope that the reader will enjoy this guide as much as we have enjoyed preparing it.

Alessandro De Maddalena, Antonella Preti & Tarik Polansky
  Milan, Italy, and San Diego, USA

Fuca Pillar at Cape Flattery, the northwest extremity of the Olympic Peninsula, Washington. Only 13 shark species have been recorded to reach the cold waters of northern Washington. *Photo courtesy of NOAA Photo Library.*

Acknowledgments

Many people have contributed to this book. We must pay special homage to Marie Levine (Global Shark Attack File, Princeton, New Jersey, USA), who took the time to write the section "The study of shark attacks" in Chapter 2.

We thank the following people for freely sharing their observations and for their assistance in assembling useful material for this book: Nicola Allegri (Italy), Roy Allen (Southwest Fisheries Science Center, NMFS, San Diego, California, USA), Greg Amptman (Undersea Discoveries, Tacoma, Washington, USA), Scot Anderson (Inverness, California, USA), Harald Bänsch (SharkProject, München, Germany), Donna Baron (Alaska State Museum, Juneau, Alaska, USA), Kurt Bergner (Hillsboro, Oregon, USA), Dianne J. Bray (Museum Victoria, Melbourne, Victoria, Australia), Dan Cartamil (Scripps Institution of Oceanography, La Jolla, California, USA), Tony Chess (Piercy, California, USA), Ann Coleman (Monterey Bay Aquarium, Monterey, California, USA), Ralph Collier (Shark Research Committee, Van Nuys, California, USA), Gianluca Cugini (Pescara, Italy), Michael Durham (Oregon Coast Aquarium, Newport, Oregon, USA), Manny Ezcurra (Monterey Bay Aquarium, Monterey, California, USA), Brooke Flammang (Lauder Lab, Department of Organismic and Evolutionary Biology, Harvard University, Cambridge, Massachusetts, USA), Kim Fulton-Bennett (Monterey Bay Aquarium Research Institute, Moss Landing, California, USA), Vittorio Gabriotti (Italian Ichthyological Society, Brescia, Italy), E. Gilat (Israel), Martin F. Gomon (Museum Victoria, Melbourne, Victoria, Australia), Chris Gotschalk (Marine Science Institute, University of California Santa Barbara, Santa Barbara, California, USA), Gavin F. Hanke (Royal British Columbia Museum, Victoria, British Columbia, Canada), Cindy Hanson (Oregon Coast Aquarium, Newport, Oregon, USA), Walter Heim (San Diego, California, USA), Henry Orr (National Marine Fisheries Service, La Jolla, California, USA), Karl Jacobson (San Jose, California, USA), Suzanne Kohin (Southwest Fisheries Science Center, La Jolla, California, USA), Bruce MacFarlane (NOAA Fisheries, California, USA), R. Aidan Martin (ReefQuest Centre for Shark Research, Vancouver, British Columbia, Canada), Gordon McFarlane (Fisheries and Oceans Canada, Pacific Biological Station, Nanaimo, British Columbia, Canada), Susan Merle (Oregon State University, Newport, Oregon, USA), Glauco Micheli

Sunset in Laredo Sound, British Columbia. Most sharks are nocturnal and mainly feed when it is dark.
Photo by Jay Lurie, courtesy of NOAA Photo Library.

(Italy), Alexia Morgan (Florida Program for Shark Research, Florida Museum of Natural History, Gainesville, Florida, USA), Lee Newman (Vancouver Aquarium, Vancouver, British Columbia, Canada), Chuck Oliver (National Marine Fisheries Service, La Jolla, California, USA), Katherine Pearson Maslenikov (University of Washington Fish Collection, School of Aquatic and Fishery Sciences, Seattle, Washington, USA), Luigi Piscitelli (Italian Ichthyological Society, Milano, Italy), Darlene Ramon (National Marine Fisheries Service, La Jolla, California, USA), John Rupp (Point Defiance Zoological Society, Tacoma, Washington, USA), Jeff Shindle (San Antonio, Texas, USA), Roxann Gess Smith (Salem, Oregon, USA), Susan E. Smith (National Marine Fisheries Service, La Jolla, California, USA), Tad Smith (Oregon Coast Aquarium, Newport, Oregon, USA), Bob Swift (Swifty's Alaskan Adventures, Valdez, Alaska, USA), Jerry Swift (Swifty's Alaskan Adventures, Valdez, Alaska, USA), Eric B. Taylor (Department of Zoology, University of British Columbia, Vancouver, British Columbia, Canada), Skip Theberge (NOAA Central Library, Silver Spring, Maryland, USA), Cindy A. Tribuzio (School of Fisheries and Ocean Sciences, University of Alaska Fairbanks, Juneau, Alaska, USA), Sean Van Sommeran (Pelagic Shark Research Foundation, Santa Cruz, California, USA), W. Waldo Wakefield (Northwest Fisheries Science Center, Fishery Resource Analysis and Monitoring Division, Newport, Oregon, USA), Nick Wegner (Southwest Fisheries Science Center, NMFS, San Diego, California, USA), Curt Whitmire (NOAA Fisheries, Northwest Fisheries Science Center, Seattle, Washington, USA), Bruce Wright (Conservation Science Institute, Wasilla, Alaska, USA), Marco Zuffa (Museo Archeologico "Luigi Donini," Ozzano dell'Emilia, Italy).

For their help, support and friendship, our sincere gratitude goes to our families, and especially to Alessandra, Antonio, Sauro, Pinuccia, Emilio, Elisabetta, Isabella, Eleonora, mamma Lidia, John Polansky, Kitti, Ming Skadaling and Seth, and also to the Mediterranean Shark Research Group and the Italian Ichthyological Society.

Our gratitude also goes to our publisher, without whom this book would not be possible.

Finally, very special thanks to Bruce Wright (Conservation Science Institute, Wasilla, Alaska, USA) and John E. Randall (Bernice P. Bishop Museum, Honolulu, Hawaii, USA) for providing the Foreword.

BEAUFORT SEA

CHUKCHI SEA

70°

BERING SEA

ALASKA

Anchorage
Prince William Sound

60°

Yakutat

Gulf of Alaska

Kodiak Island

Alexander Archipelago

BRITISH COLUMBIA

Queen Charlotte Islands

Aleutian Islands

50°

PACIFIC OCEAN

Vancouver

Vancouver Island

WA

150°   160°   150°   140°   130°   120°

Chapter 1

Biology, Ethology and Ecology of Sharks

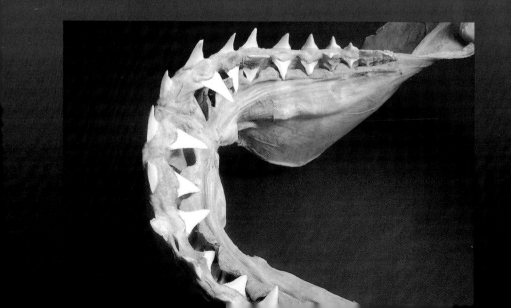

CLASSIFICATION

Sharks belong to the Phylum Chordata, the Subphylum Vertebrata, the Class Chondrichthyes, the Subclass Elasmobranchii and the Superorder Selachimorpha. Sharks, together with rays and chimaeras, are called Chondrichthyes or cartilaginous fishes. These fishes have skeletons composed of cartilage, a light and flexible tissue that is present even in the human skeleton; in fact the only bony tissues present in the shark body are found in its teeth and scales. Osteichthyes, also known as bony fish or teleosts, have skeletons made of bone.

Opposite inset: Great white jaw (carchardon carcharias) Photo by Alessandro De Maddalena.

Sharks are classified into eight orders: Hexanchiformes (frilled and cow sharks), Squaliformes (dogfish sharks), Pristiophoriformes (saw sharks), Squatiniformes (angelsharks), Heterodontiformes (bullhead sharks), Orectolobiformes (carpet sharks), Lamniformes (mackerel sharks) and Carcharhiniformes (ground sharks). These orders are divided in 34 families that include 479 species of sharks. With the discovery of unknown species and a wider knowledge of sharks' morphology, this classification is changing continuously.

A white-spotted ratfish *(Hydrolagus colliei)* photographed off Three Tree Point in Puget Sound, Washington. The white-spotted ratfish belongs to the Subclass Holocephali (chimaeras). *Photo by Greg Amptman.*

EVOLUTION

Sharks came into being some 400 million years ago. This event occurred between the Silurian and the Early Devonian periods. Sharks most likely evolved from the placoderms, a group of extinct armored bony fishes. Large numbers of shark fossils have been found in the world, but, although shark vertebrae can occasionally be preserved as fossils because of their partial calcification, complete skeletons are preserved only in very rare cases. The reason for this is that the cartilaginous skeleton rapidly disintegrates after a shark dies. On the other hand, shark teeth fossilize easily because they are highly calcified. So fossil teeth are extremely numerous but very often they are the only remains of an extinct species.

Sharks have not changed much during the last 100 million years. This fact suggests that these creatures developed characteristics early on in their evolutionary history that have made them very well adapted to their environment. Consequently, we can consider sharks as a highly evolved group.

SIZE

The smallest shark found on the coast of the Pacific Northwest is the brown catshark (*Apristurus brunneus*). It hatches at about 7 cm (2.75 in) in length and rarely grows up to be more than 68 cm (26.5 in). Although it is commonly believed that all sharks are large, most are in fact quite small—and do not exceed 1.5 m (5 ft) in length. Other sharks, however, are massive in length. In the study area there are nine very large shark species that have been confirmed to exceed 3 m (10 ft) in length. They are the basking shark (*Cetorhinus maximus*), the great white shark (*Carcharodon carcharias*), the common thresher shark (*Alopias vulpinus*), the bluntnose sixgill shark (*Hexanchus griseus*), the shortfin mako (*Isurus oxyrinchus*), the Pacific sleeper shark (*Somniosus pacificus*), the prickly shark (*Echinorhinus cookei*), the blue shark (*Prionace glauca*) and the salmon shark (*Lamna ditropis*). The basking shark is the second-largest living fish, attaining lengths of at least 9.8 m (32 ft) and up to 12 m (40 ft). Only the whale shark (*Rhincodon typus*), which can grow up to 20 m (65.5 ft), is larger (but it is not present in the Pacific Northwest). Excluding the basking shark, which feeds on plankton, the largest predator species (meaning an animal that catches, kills and eats large prey) is the great white shark.

A fossil tooth of the extinct megatooth shark (*Carcharodon megalodon*) that reached 15 m (50 ft) in length. *Photo by Alessandro De Maddalena.*

Below:
Bluntnose sixgill shark (*Hexanchus griseus*). *Photo © www.davidfleetham.com.*

An estimated 5-m (16-ft) great white shark *(Carcharodon carcharias)*, caught probably in the early 20th century off Newport, Oregon. *Photo courtesy of Roxann Gess Smith.*

It has been confirmed to attain at least 6.6 m (21.5 ft) in length, but it is estimated to exceed 8 m (26 ft). Female sharks attain larger maximum sizes than males.

MORPHOLOGY, SWIMMING AND BUOYANCY

Body shape varies considerably among species of sharks. Most of these fishes have a streamlined body, a long, flattened snout, a ventral parabolic mouth and an asymmetric caudal fin with the upper lobe much longer than the lower lobe. However, body shape is related to each species' habitat and way of life. For example, the benthic brown catshark (*Apristurus brunneus*) is long and slender; the pelagic, fast-swimming shortfin mako (*Isurus oxyrinchus*) has a highly pronounced spindle shape; and the benthic Pacific angelshark (*Squatina californica*) is considerably flattened. "Benthic" refers to animals living on the sea bottom, and "pelagic" to those living in the open sea.

The fins of a shark are fundamental in swimming. Most species have eight fins: a pair of pectoral fins, a pair of pelvic fins, a first dorsal fin, a second dorsal fin, an anal and a caudal fin. The caudal fin is used for propulsion: the shark swims by moving its caudal fin from side to side. The longer upper caudal fin lobe drives the shark down while swimming, but this is balanced by a lift generated by the flattened head and the almost horizontally wide pectoral fins. In some benthic species, such as the brown catshark, the lower lobe is almost absent,

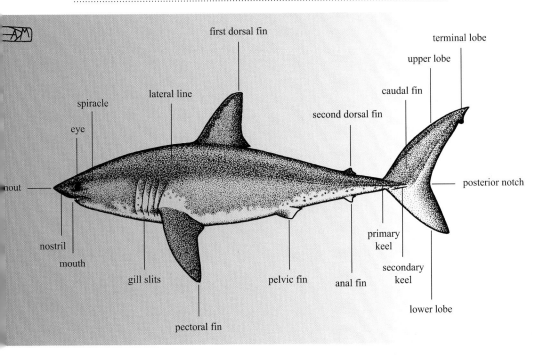

The external anatomy of the salmon shark *(Lamna ditropis)*. *Drawing by Alessandro De Maddalena.*

while in some fast-swimming species, such as the salmon shark (*Lamna ditropis*), the upper and lower lobes are nearly equal in size, while the snout is conical. In some sharks the hydrodynamic design is improved by lateral keels on the sides of their caudal peduncle that are flattened and laterally expanded. Usually there is one pair of caudal keels, but the salmon shark has two pairs of caudal keels (the second pair is much smaller and located on the sides of the caudal fin, immediately below the caudal peduncle). The fastest species may be the shortfin mako, with maximum speeds of 35–56 km per hour (22–35 mph). However, sharks usually swim slowly and even the fastest species have a relatively low average speed.

Some sharks have a spine before the dorsal fins, such as the piked dogfish (*Squalus acanthias*), and can use these dorsal fin spines as a defense against predators. The section of the dorsal fin spine has been useful in studying the age of the piked dogfish and other species.

Most bony fishes have a gas bladder. This is a gas-filled sac lying in the upper part of the body cavity to offset the weight of heavier tissues such as bone. Sharks lack a gas bladder, but because of the light cartilaginous skeleton and a huge oily liver with a very low specific

The caudal fin is used for propulsion. Of the 18 shark species known to occur in the Pacific Northwest, the salmon shark *(Lamna ditropis)* is one of the most frequently observed. *Painting by Alessandro De Maddalena.*

gravity, they are only slightly heavier than sea water. Certain species have developed additional ways of reducing their total weight; for example, the blue shark (*Prionace glauca*) has a low-density jelly in its snout. The difference in the density of various sharks is also related to their habitat. Pelagic species are less dense than benthic species. In general, sharks have to constantly swim to keep from sinking to the bottom of the ocean floor. However, many sharks, particularly those that are benthic, lie on the sea bottom for long periods; typical examples include the Pacific angelshark, which lies buried in the sand for a long time waiting for prey.

A shark's skin is specifically designed to improve hydrodynamics. The skin is rough and abrasive because it is covered by very small to moderately large structures called "dermal denticles" or "placoid scales." These dermal denticles are actually modified teeth rather than true scales. A denticle is composed of a pulp, dentine and enamel-like vitrodentine over a bony basal plate or root that is set into the skin. Dermal denticles give the shark skin its sandpaper texture, and they reduce friction during swimming. The shape of dermal denticles varies from species to species and from body part to body part. Therefore their shape is also of importance in the identification of a species, especially when it is not possible to examine the whole specimen, such as in fish markets where sharks are often brought already cut into pieces.

MOUTH AND TEETH

Mouth size, tooth shape and jaw morphology are well adapted to the prey that is available to each shark species. In almost all sharks the mouth is located on the undersurface of its head (except the angelshark, which has a terminal mouth) and varies in size, from small to very large, and in shape, from parabolic to almost straight. Usually there are upper and lower labial furrows at the corners of the mouth that can be very short to very long (in the smoothhounds, length is useful to help in species identification). Jaws vary considerably in size.

Alessandro De Maddalena showing the jaws of a large shortfin mako *(Isurus oxyrinchus)*. *Photo by Nicola Allegri.*

Some sharks have spectacularly wide jaws, for example, the basking shark (*Cetorhinus maximus*) and the great white shark (*Carcharodon carcharias*).

Sharks' jaws seem to have been derived from a modification of the first gill arch. In the most primitive sharks, the cladodonts, the mouth was terminal rather than ventral, and the jaws were long—the upper jaw being fixed tightly to the chondrocranium (braincase). This kind of jaw suspension is called "amphistylic" and allowed little independent movement. With "hyostylic" jaw suspension the jaws are shorter, allowing the upper jaw to lose its tight connection to the chondrocranium and become loosely suspended from it. This makes the upper jaw highly mobile and enables the shark to protrude it. Most modern sharks have a hyostylic jaw suspension.

The mouth's ventral position does not impede a shark's ability to feed. Snout elevation and upper jaw protrusion carry the mouth in an almost terminal position. The best example is the great white shark. Its bite action consists of a sequence of jaw and snout movements: a) snout lift, b) lower jaw depression, c) upper jaw protrusion, d) lower jaw elevation, e) snout drop. The great white shark removes large chunks of prey by biting and shaking its head laterally (large specimens can easily remove 20 kg/45 lbs of flesh in a single bite).

Shark teeth are modified and enlarged dermal denticles; consequently, they are composed of a pulp, dentine and enamel-like vitrodentine over a bony base. Each tooth has a root and a crown and the projection of the crown is called the cusp. Many species have teeth with a large main cusp flanked by one or more auxiliary cusplets. A few, such as the bluntnose sixgill shark (*Hexanchus griseus*), are provided with a row of cusps on a single tooth. The tooth is not fixed into a socket but is implanted with the root in the connective tissue (tooth bed) of the jaw. Sharks' teeth are often broken and easily detached, but these fishes have a perfect system of regular tooth replacement. Teeth are formed in a groove along the inner jaw, and behind the front teeth there are several parallel rows of replacement teeth, with 5 to 15 rows in each jaw. Teeth are continuously replaced throughout a shark's lifespan; in whaler sharks (*Carcharhinus sp.*), each tooth is replaced every 8 to 15 days during the first year of life, but in adults replacement slows to probably every month. Sharks with small teeth usually have more than one functional row in the jaw while species with large teeth usually have one or two functional rows.

The number of teeth on the outer row of the upper and lower jaws is used to help identify species. The dental formula is used in order to present the number of teeth in a shark's mouth. For example, the great white shark's dental formula is usually 13–13/11–11. This dental formula is read as 13 teeth in the right side of the upper jaw—13 teeth in the left side of the upper jaw / 11 teeth in the right side of the lower jaw—11 teeth in the left side of the lower jaw. Moreover the dental formula often shows a certain variability. For example, a great white shark's formula has a variability of 12 to 14–12 to 14/10 to 13–10 to 13.

Teeth are an invaluable means of identification, and exhibit a wide variety of shapes between species according to what they eat. There are three main tooth shapes common to sharks with similar feeding ecologies:

Functional front teeth and rows of replacement teeth in the lower jaw of a great white shark (*Carcharodon carcharias*). *Photo by Alessandro De Maddalena.*

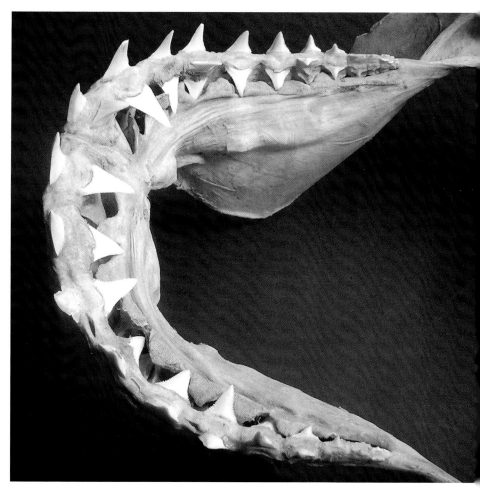

a) teeth adapted for shearing or sawing pieces from large animals such as large fishes and marine mammals: these teeth are large, triangular, sharp, with or without serrate edges; for example, the great white shark (*Carcharodon carcharias*);

b) teeth adapted for seizing smaller, faster moving prey such as small schools of fish: these teeth are narrow and curved and tend to be moderate in size to very long; for example, the shortfin mako (*Isurus oxyrinchus*);

c) teeth adapted for crushing hard prey such as molluscs and crustaceans: these teeth are smooth or arranged in a pavement formation; for example, the smoothhounds (*Mustelus spp.*).

Shark teeth, however, have been modified in a number of ways. In most species the teeth of the upper jaw are very different in shape from those of the lower jaw: teeth in the lower jaw are often smaller and narrower. Anterior teeth are larger than the teeth that follow them. Teeth vary considerably in size from species to species. Some have spectacularly enlarged teeth, such as the great white shark and

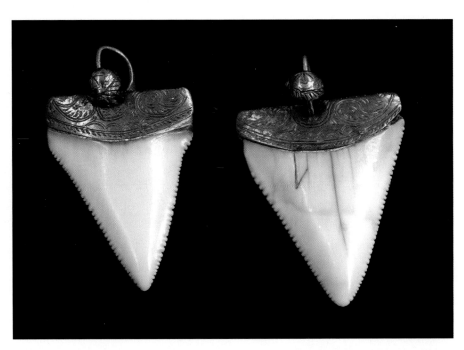

Earrings made of white shark *(Carcharodon carcharias)* teeth (Alaska State Museum, Juneau, cat. no. II-B-981), banded both front and back at the root end by a wide crescent-shaped band of gold, held on by tiny rivets and solder. The bands are engraved with flowing, scroll-like lines. Fasteners are silver, jointed, and fasten in the front under a knob of engraved silver. *Photo courtesy of Alaska State Museum.*

the shortfin mako: the largest great white shark tooth measured 6.4 cm (2.5 in).

Tooth shape is also related to a shark's age; it alters its tooth shape as it grows larger and changes its diet. In order for the shortfin mako to eat fast pelagic fishes, it is born with narrow teeth, but as it grows these become thick and strong to accommodate larger prey such as swordfish (*Xiphias gladius*) and small cetaceans. Young specimens are sometimes mistaken for other shark species because of their tooth shape. For example, young salmon shark teeth are sometimes mistaken for those of shortfin makos because they lack cusplets, and young white sharks' teeth can be mistaken for those of salmon sharks because they have small cusplets and partially lack serrated edges.

The Tlingit are the northernmost of the Northwest Coast peoples, who range from southern Alaska to the coast of Oregon. They lived traditionally by fishing and hunting marine animals and built large plank houses, totem poles and ocean-going dugout canoes. To this day, the livelihood of the Tlingit continues to be linked to the bounty of the natural world. The people maintain interests in both fishing and forestry. Earrings made of large shark teeth were worn by high-ranking Tlingit men during ceremonies. *Shax'dax'ooxu* is the Tlingit term for shark-tooth earrings.

RESPIRATION

The respiratory organs of sharks are the gills. While a bony fish's gills are covered by a flap called the operculum, a shark's gill slits are uncovered, making them external and clearly visible. Sharks have five to seven pairs of gill slits. In the Pacific Northwest there is only one species that has seven pairs of gill slits, the broadnose sevengill shark (*Notorynchus cepedianus*), and one species that has six, the bluntnose sixgill shark (*Hexanchus griseus*), while all others have five. A shark's mouth leads to the buccal cavity and to the pharynx, where gills are located. Oxygen is extracted from the water and carbon dioxide is released due to highly vascularized membranes called gill lamellae. Moreover, many sharks have two small openings located behind or below the eyes, one per side, called the spiracles. These are rudimentary gill openings and are used as entrance for water instead of the mouth. These openings are especially useful in those species that live on the sea bottom; therefore, the spiracles are larger in benthic species such as the Pacific angelshark (*Squatina californica*) and very small

An estimated 3-m (10-ft) bluntnose sixgill shark *(Hexanchus griseus)* photographed off Owens Beach, in Puget Sound, Washington. Almost all sharks have five pairs of gill slits. In the waters of the Pacific Northwest the bluntnose sixgill shark is the only species that has six pairs of gill slits. The spiracles are small in this species.
Photo by Greg Amptman.

in pelagic species such as the common thresher shark (*Alopias vulpinus*), or even totally absent, such as in the blue shark (*Prionace glauca*). Fast pelagic sharks, like the shortfin mako (*Isurus oxyrinchus*) require a larger amount of oxygen; therefore, they have to constantly swim to stay alive.

CIRCULATION

Sharks have a simple circulatory system. The heart is divided into two parts, the auricle and the ventricle. First, the blood goes from the ventricle to the ventral aorta. It then moves into the branchial arteries and then to the capillaries located in the gills (where gaseous exchanges occur and the blood becomes oxygenated). The blood then moves onto the dorsal aorta, and continues through the rest of the body via smaller arteries. After the oxygen and nutrients have been delivered to the organs by the capillaries, the blood enters in the venous system and then returns to the heart primarily via the cardinal veins.

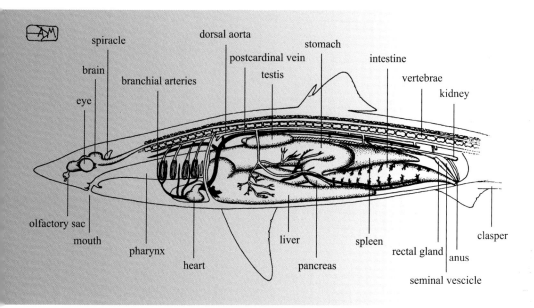

Internal anatomy of a piked dogfish *(Squalus acanthias)*. Drawing by Alessandro De Maddalena.

While most sharks have body temperatures equal to that of the surrounding sea water, some species of the Order Lamniformes exhibit regional endothermy: this means that they maintain a higher body temperature than that of the sea water because of a heat-retaining system. Off the coasts of Oregon, Washington, British Columbia and Alaska, the species that show endothermy are the shortfin mako (*Isurus oxyrinchus*), great white shark (*Carcharodon carcharias*), salmon shark (*Lamna ditropis*) and the common thresher shark (*Alopias vulpinus*). Red muscles are the most powerful during swimming. Endothermic sharks have larger amounts of red muscle tissue sited deep in the trunk, close to the vertebral column, while on other species, these muscles are more superficially located. The red muscle tissue is connected to the circulatory system by a complicated network of arteries and veins called the *rete mirabile*. As heat is generated in the red muscles by swimming, warm blood passes through the venules into the *rete mirabile*. The heat is then transferred to the parallel arteries, and heat is conserved in the shark's body rather than dissipating to the en-

A salmon shark *(Lamna ditropis)*. This shark is a particularly powerful swimmer because it is among those few sharks that are able to maintain a higher body temperature than the sea water, thanks to their physiological heat-retaining systems. *Photo by Scot Anderson.*

vironment. Heat is a form of energy, hence warm-blooded sharks have more energy at their disposal and are very powerful, fast and able to leap from the sea's surface. The metabolism of these very active species requires a large amount of oxygen, so their gill slits are long.

DIGESTIVE SYSTEM

Similar to that of other vertebrates, a shark's digestion takes place in the mouth, stomach and intestine. The food enters the stomach, where it is acted on by the digestive juices. A shark's stomach is very large, which enables these formidable predators to ingest whole animals, large chunks of prey and a large amount of smaller prey. Consequently sharks are able to consume large amounts of food at any one time and don't need to feed often. Sharks are able to evert their stomachs, possibly to provide a means for them to eliminate indigestible objects.

The products of digestion are absorbed in the relatively short intestine. In most species the intestine is called the spiral valve because its internal surface resembles a spiral staircase. This form provides the maximum absorptive area in a small space, allowing more room for a large stomach and liver.

Studies have shown that sharks' digestion is slow compared to that of bony fishes. In fact, initial digestion of the food is relatively fast, taking around 24 hours, but usually it takes at least a day and a half to five days for the food to be completely voided. The gastric evacuation rate was estimated for piked dogfish (*Squalus acanthias*) from Puget Sound, Washington. The amount of time required for an average meal to be evacuated is four and a half days. The rate at which food is digested is closely related to the activity level of each species and its physiology.

A shark's stomach is very large, allowing a species such as the great white shark (*Carcharodon carcharias*) to ingest enormous prey (like that of a swordfish or tuna) whole or in large pieces. *Photo by Vittorio Gabriotti.*

REPRODUCTION

Sharks live fairly long lives. Most species live about 12 to 27 years, but there are particular species, such as the piked dogfish (*Squalus acanthias*), that have a maximum life span of at least 40 years and possibly up to about 100 years. Sharks have a slow rate of growth and

The claspers can be clearly seen in the pelvic region of this male broadnose sevengill shark *(Notorynchus cepedianus)*. Photo by Cindy Hanson, courtesy of Oregon Coast Aquarium.

consequently they have also long sexual maturation times. In fact, depending on the species, a shark can reach sexual maturity in 2 to 20 years.

Sharks have internal fertilization. The males are provided with two organs called claspers: these are located at the base of the pelvic fins and serve to impregnate females. In young specimens the claspers are short and soft, while in adult specimens they become calcified and long (consequently the sex of a shark is easy to identify depending on the presence or the absence of the claspers). During mating, the male inserts one clasper into the female's cloaca. In order to stimulate the female to copulate, often the male bites the female both during courtship and copulation. Consequently scars called "love bites" or mating scars can be seen on the bodies (flanks, gill region, belly, back, caudal peduncle and fins) of female specimens.

Three different reproductive methods have been observed in sharks:

• oviparity: the female lays horny egg cases containing embryos nourished by their yolk sac;

• aplacental viviparity: the female produces live young nourished in the uterus by a yolk sac;

• placental viviparity: the female produces live young nourished in the uterus by a placenta formed by a modified yolk sac attached to the uterine wall.

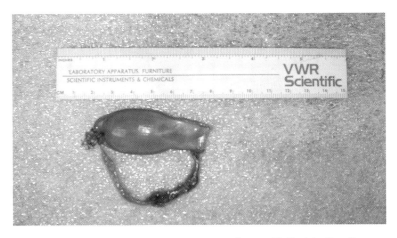

In oviparous species the female lays horny egg cases containing embryos nourished by their yolk sac. The photo shows a brown catshark *(Apristurus brunneus)* egg case preserved in the University of Washington Fish Collection (catalog number UW 029664). *Photo by Katherine Pearson Maslenikov, courtesy of the University of Washington Fish Collection.*

Aplacental viviparity is the most common reproductive method. In some aplacental viviparous sharks, two particular methods of nourishing the embryos have been observed. In the oophagy, embryos in the uterus also feed on additional unfertilized eggs produced by their mother. In the embryophagy, also called intrauterine cannibalism, embryos in the uterus also feed on their siblings.

A shark's gestation period is among the longest of any living vertebrate. The average gestation is 9 to 12 months, but it is up to 24 months in the piked dogfish (*Squalus acanthias*), and it has been hypothesized that it could reach about 3 years in the basking shark (*Cetorhinus maximus*). Many sharks may reproduce only every other year. Litter sizes of sharks occurring in Pacific Northwest waters vary from 1 to a maximum of 135 in the blue shark (*Prionace glauca*), but most species produce relatively small numbers of young. Assuming that the salmon shark (*Lamna ditropis*) has an annual reproductive cycle, it is estimated that a female salmon shark would probably give birth to roughly 70 young during her lifetime.

When pups are born, they are fully formed and able to live and catch prey without any assistance from their mother. Many shark species segregate by sex and size. Nursery areas—often coastal waters, lagoons or estuaries—where only newborns and juveniles live, have been observed for several species. The existence of these areas reduces the risk of cannibalism; moreover, here the pups usually find a greater abundance of suitable prey.

SENSES

Sharks have a highly developed nervous system and sense organs that are used to find prey. They have four senses: chemoreception (smell and taste), mechanoreception (touching and hearing), photo-reception (vision), and electroreception (ability to sense electric fields).

Feeding areas are often located via olfaction. The nostrils are located on the underside of the snout and lead to the olfactory bulb. Sharks have a keen sense of smell: for example, the slick produced by a large cetacean carcass attracts large sharks such as blue sharks (*Prionace glauca*) and white sharks (*Carcharodon carcharias*) from a long distance. Some species of sharks follow the scent by criss-crossing the odor trail, while others swim upstream against the odor. Stimulated by blood and food in the water, a shark's behavior becomes increasingly aggressive.

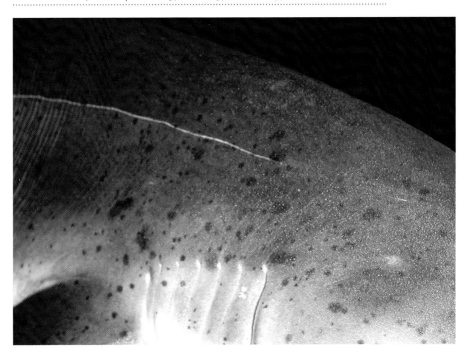

The lateral line system and the ears give sharks the ability to detect movements in the water. The lateral line is a row of sensory receptors located along the flanks and head and is pressure-sensitive, enabling the shark to detect water vibrations—both direction and the amount of movement—from great distances. A wounded creature, a speared fish for example, sends vibrations to the predator that indicate the animal is in trouble and therefore easy prey; these vibrations soon attract sharks. These predators also use this sense to detect water currents. Sharks have two inner ears connected to the exterior by narrow canals called endolymphatic ducts. A shark's hearing is related to the lateral line system, and is very sensitive to low-frequency vibrations, like those produced by bleeding prey.

The lateral line is evident in this broadnose sevengill shark (Notorynchus cepedianus). Photo by Roy Allen; courtesy of NMFS.

Prey detection depends heavily on vision. Sharks' vision is excellent. Different parts of their retinas are adapted for bright and dim light, consequently sharks are able to use their eyes even in poor light. The retina contains cone and rod photoreceptors (cones function in bright light while rods function in dim light). The tapetum lucidum is a structure that lies under the retina and reflects incoming light back through the retina to restimulate photoreceptors, thus increasing the sensitivity of the eye. At least some sharks have color vision.

The eyes of a piked dogfish *(Squalus acanthias)*, above, and a tope shark *(Galeorhinus galeus)*, below, reflect light. The tapetum lucidum is a structure that lies under the retina and reflects incoming light back through the retina to restimulate photoreceptors, thus increasing the sensitivity of the eye. *Photo by Cindy Hanson, courtesy of Oregon Coast Aquarium.*

A salmon shark *(Lamna ditropis)* hooked off Newport, Oregon, rolls its eyes backwards. This species lacks the nictitating membrane, so it rolls the eyes backwards when something may endanger it. *Photo by Kurt Bergner, courtesy of Karl Jacobson.*

Sharks have immovable eyelids, but many species have a third eyelid called the nictitating membrane, formed by an additional fold on the lower eyelid. This structure is movable and when the shark is feeding, the membrane closes over it for protection. However, many species lack the nictitating membrane: the great white shark is among these, and in order to reduce the risk of injury, it rolls the eyes backwards during attack on a prey.

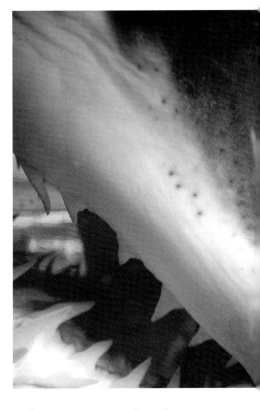

At close range, sharks can detect the minute electrical currents generated by the nervous systems of their prey by using electrical sensors called the ampullae of Lorenzini. The ampullae are numerous small organs containing a sensory hair cell filled with an electrically conductive jelly. The external openings of electroreceptors are small pores located over the head and particularly abundant on the underside of the snout. These sophisticated sensors are very useful in finding prey buried under sand, but sharks also use this sense to orient using the earth's magnetic field. It is because of the ampullae of Lorenzini that sharks are also attracted to metals—a response to the galvanic currents produced by electrochemical interactions between sea water and metals.

The external openings of the ampullae of Lorenzini on the head of a short-fin mako (*Isurus oxyrinchus*). *Photo by Alessandro De Maddalena.*

Touch receptors are located all over the shark's body. This sense is used to obtain further information by bumping its prey. Taste enables the predator to discriminate food before it is ingested: some sharks, for example the great white shark, decide a food's palatability while it is lodged in their mouths. Gustatory receptors are located in the shark's mouth and in the rest of the pharynx.

COLOR

Sharks' bodies are almost always dark on the dorsal surfaces (usually gray, brown, dark green or blue) and white on the ventral

surfaces. This color pattern serves to render these fishes invisible both to their prey and to their predators, and from above and below. The fins often show a different coloration at their apex and posterior margin, usually being dark, light, black or white. Some species show dark or light spots on the body, such as the broadnose sevengill shark (*Notorynchus cepedianus*), and in the case of the Pacific angelshark (*Squatina californica*) the spotted pattern is useful as camouflage on the sandy sea floor. A more complex color pattern is by far less common, but can be found in the leopard shark (*Triakis semifasciata*). Rare cases of albinism have been recorded in a few shark species: among those that occur in the Pacific Northwest are the basking shark (*Cetorhinus maximus*), great white shark (*Carcharodon carcharias*) and tope shark (*Galeorhinus galeus*).

The coloration of the leopard shark (*Triakis semifasciata*), grayish brown with large, dark saddle marks and spots, makes its identification immediate. *Photo by Harald Bänsch.*

DISTRIBUTION AND HABITAT

Most sharks favor tropical or temperate waters, therefore it is not surprising that in the Pacific Northwest a total of 18 shark species (a relatively low number) have been recorded to date. In general, the farther north we move, the fewer number of shark species we encounter. Only 13 shark species have been recorded to reach the cold waters of northern Washington and up through the Strait of Juan de Fuca, and only 11 species have been recorded to reach the icy waters of Alaska.

Sharks may be found in all the northeastern Pacific Ocean and on any type of sea floor. In the area large sharks usually stay offshore; some prefer the area close to shoals or the straits where they can easily find more prey. In very rare cases, these fishes venture into shallow waters; it happens only occasionally, especially if the shoreline is located very close to a zone where the bottom suddenly becomes deeper. Most sharks live or pass most of their time on continental and insular shelves and upper slopes; however, we also know that some of these predators, such as the bluntnose sixgill shark (*Hexanchus griseus*), Pacific sleeper shark (*Somniosus pacificus*) and longnose catshark (*Apristurus kampae*) can visit the deeper parts of the sea.

The Aleutian Islands. Only 11 shark species have been recorded to reach the icy waters of Alaska. *Photo by Harley D. Nygren, courtesy of NOAA Photo Library.*

The Pacific sleeper shark (*Somniosus pacificus*) is a giant of the deep waters. It has a maximum length of at least 430 cm (169 in) and reaches depths of 1,975 m (6,480 ft). *Painting by Alessandro De Maddalena.*

41

The shortfin mako (*Isurus oxyrinchus*) is a very active species and therefore consumes more food than other species. *Photo by Jeff Shindle.*

FEEDING

Sharks consume a small amount of food, the average meal being 3–5 percent of their body weight. They feed intensively for a short time and then feed very little for a longer period of time. Most sharks feed at one- or two-day intervals and are also able to stop feeding for several weeks. During this time they live off the oil reserves in their large livers. Researchers estimated that a 4.6-m (15-ft) great white shark (*Carcharodon carcharias*) could survive a month and a half after a complete meal. Obviously food consumption is related to the activity level of a given species, so the food consumption per day is different for each species. Sedentary sharks require a small amount of food, while more active species such as the blue shark (*Prionace glauca*) consume more, and some very active warm-blooded species such as the shortfin mako (*Isurus oxyrinchus*), even more.

Most sharks are nocturnal and mainly feed when it is dark; however, daytime feeding by nocturnal species is often reported (even these sharks will eat when the opportunity presents itself). Other species, such as the great white shark, hunt during both the daytime and nighttime. Certain species are vertical migrators on a diel cycle; they stay in deep zones during the day and ascend to the surface at night to feed. Examples of such sharks found in the area are bluntnose sixgill sharks (*Hexanchus griseus*) and Pacific sleeper sharks (*Somniosus pacificus*).

Sharks usually inflict deep wounds on their prey. The prey are often found stranded dead or alive or observed floating at the sea's surface with the wide marks of an attack on their bodies. Sometimes tooth enamel fragments are found in the carcasses. Bite scars are frequently found on tunas, swordfishes and dolphins. These animals are often thought to have been hit by a boat, because the lacerations are similar to those caused by boat propellers. Bite scars and fresh wounds are used to identify species of sharks responsible for predation and scavenging on various animals, however, the proper identification is not easy.

DIET

Most sharks have no enemies except for other sharks and man. They are carnivorous and feed on a wide variety of prey of comparable or smaller size to themselves, most feeding mainly on live prey, some attacking healthy prey and some typically feeding on diseased, wounded or dead animals. Sharks eat bony fishes, cartilaginous fishes, molluscs, crustaceans, echinoderms, worms, pinnipeds, cetaceans, marine turtles, sea snakes, sea birds and even planktonic organisms such as euphasiids, copepods and jellyfishes.

Many sharks are opportunistic feeders: they can feed on diverse species depending on their availability in a given area, and when a

This close-up of a big skate (*Raja binoculata*) was shot at The Lobster Shop Wall in Tacoma, Washington. Broadnose sevengill sharks (*Notorynchus cepedianus*) are known predators of these skates. *Photo by Greg Amptman.*

prey is scarce they feed on other species. A particularly common species or one that is easily captured may dominate the diet of the opportunistic sharks. There are also numerous sharks that show dietary preferences and some species that have a highly specialized diet. The common thresher (*Alopias vulpinus*) feeds mainly on anchovies, hakes and mackerels, while the great white sharks (*Carcharodon carcharias*) and blue sharks (*Prionace glauca*) seem to feed selectively on the energy-rich blubber layer when scavenging a whale carcass.

The examination of shark stomachs has shown that for most species about 70–80 percent of the diet consists of bony fishes. Salmon is the major prey item of salmon sharks (*Lamna ditropis*) in subarctic waters. In 1989, the estimated number of salmon sharks in the north Pacific Ocean was at least 2 million. From spring to autumn 1989, salmon sharks aged five years or over occurring in subarctic waters appear to have consumed 12.6–25.2 percent of the total annual run of Pacific salmon.

Many sharks seem to prefer cartilaginous fishes to bony fishes, with elasmobranchs and rays being the most important prey to many species. A large number of sharks also eat a certain percentage of invertebrates, especially cephalopods and crustaceans. Crustaceans are a very important prey for the brown catshark (*Apristurus brunneus*). Cephalopods, on the other hand, form the main item in the diet of the blue shark and young bluntnose sixgill sharks (*Hexanchus griseus*).

Some sharks feed on marine mammals, but while a few species

A shark attack on a white-sided dolphin *(Lagenorynchus obliquidens)* has been recorded in Oregon waters. *Photo by Budd Christman, NOAA Corps / courtesy of NOAA Photo Library.*

such as the great white shark and tiger shark (*Galeocerdo cuvier*) feed on both live and dead specimens, most sharks eat these animals only when found dead. Large cetacean carcasses are a common food source for species such as the oceanic whitetip shark *(Carcharhinus longimanus)* and the blue shark. A few sharks also eat a small percentage of marine turtles and sea birds. In the waters of the Pacific Northwest there are even plankton eaters such as the basking sharks (*Cetorhinus maximus*).

Diet is also related to a shark's age and size. There is considerable variation in the diet of many sharks as they grow, with larger prey becoming increasingly important. Variation in the diet is accompanied by changes in tooth shape, so whereas many young sharks feed mainly on bony fishes and molluscs, when they attain larger sizes they begin eating larger prey such as cartilaginous fishes and marine mammals.

There is also considerable variation in the diet of several sharks from one location or season to the next. Regional differences in the diet are attributable to the higher availability of particular prey as many sharks focus their hunting activity on the locale's most abundant species.

A harbor seal (*Phoca vitulina richardii*) in North Puget Sound, Washington. White shark predation on harbor seals has been recorded in British Columbia and Alaska waters. *Photo courtesy of NOAA Photo Library / Padilla Bay National Estuarine Research Reserve.*

MUTUALISMS

The relationship between two individuals belonging to different species, where both organisms benefit from the relationship, is called a "mutualism." The relationships between pilot fishes (family Carangidae) and sharks and between remoras (family Echeneidae) and sharks are cases of mutualism. The remora has a dorsal suction disk (formed from its modified dorsal fin) that is used to attach itself to sharks, mantas, marine turtles and other large animals, but it uses this organ only when the large animal changes direction or slows down. The pilot fish (*Naucrates ductor*) is frequently observed close to large cartilaginous fishes, bony fishes and marine turtles. Remoras and pilot fishes benefit from their relationship with sharks by eating the sharks' food scraps or excrements and parasites (sharks are hosts to several external parasites), as well as by riding sharks' bow waves. Sharks, on the other hand, benefit from these relationships by being cleaned of parasites.

The great white shark (*Carcharodon carcharias*) dominates the blue shark (*Prionace glauca*) when both species are feeding. *Painting by Alessandro De Maddalena.*

BEHAVIOR

Until recently, the behavior of these predators has remained es-

sentially unknown. Slowly we are filling in the gaps in regards to this fundamental aspect of sharks.

Most sharks hunt alone but they can also be found in pairs or in small or large groups, as is the case with the piked dogfish (*Squalus acanthias*). Many behaviors have a communication function. These predators often attempt to communicate with animals (man included) using particular signals before executing an attack. These behaviors may function as a means of defending the shark itself, its pups or its individual territory. Consequently, many accidents can be avoided with the correct interpretation of a shark's behavior, particularly the threat displays. Often the shark circles the prey or even bumps it before attacking. The great white shark (*Carcharodon carcharias*) and the shortfin mako (*Isurus oxyrinchus*) show a threat display with a partial opening of the jaws; the shortfin mako also swims rapidly in a figure eight pattern.

Sometimes, when two great white sharks attempt to feed on a single carcass, one will raise its caudal fin above the water and slap the surface, splashing the water toward the other shark. This behavior has been interpreted as an agonistic display—one shark trying to force the competitor to flee to avoid a fight. Many sharks eat other shark species as well as members of their own species, therefore social hierarchies serve as an anti-predatory tactic on the part of the subordinate shark. These hierarchies are size-dependent: smaller individuals move away from larger individuals. Social hierarchies between different species and among members of the same species have been reported when sharks are feeding. The great white sharks dominate blue sharks (*Prionace glauca*) when both species are feeding (blue sharks will not scavenge on a whale carcass when white sharks are feeding on it).

The study of the behavior of sharks has revealed that these fishes have developed a wide variety of predatory strategies. Many active sharks, such as the shortfin mako, often pursue their prey by simply swimming rapidly to capture it; others attack violently and by surprise like the great white shark, which performs horizontal- or vertical-oriented attacks on its prey by swimming fast from deep waters without warning; others, such as the Pacific angelshark (*Squatina californica*), lie motionless on the sea bottom and wait for passing prey, then strike suddenly and very rapidly. Other species have developed particular strategies to feed on schooling prey; for example, the common thresher shark (*Alopias vulpinus*) slashes the water with the incredibly

The Pacific angelshark (*Squatina californica*) lies motionless on the sea bottom and waits for passing prey, then strikes suddenly and very rapidly. *Photo by Tony Chess.*

long upper lobe of its caudal fins in order to herd and disorient the fishes. Blue sharks, on the other hand, simply swim through masses of squids with their mouths wide open and ingest the squids that inadvertently swim into their jaws. However, no shark relies exclusively on a single tactic to capture its prey.

THE ECOLOGICAL IMPORTANCE OF SHARKS

Sharks are at the top of most marine food chains. Consequently, they play an important ecological role in marine communities. These fishes, as predators and scavengers, are fundamental instruments of natural selection. They contribute to the stability of marine ecosystems and maintain biodiversity. Sharks have a substantial impact on prey organisms, therefore shark predation is an important natural control on the population size of many marine species. Knowing the diet and biology of sharks is essential to understanding the effect these predators have on marine ecosystems.

To be located at the top of the food chain means to have almost no enemy. Their eggs and young are susceptible to a very restricted range of predators including some fishes and molluscs, and only a few crea-

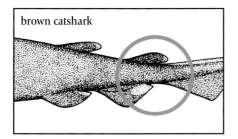

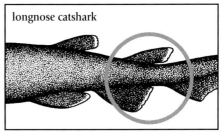

Prickly shark (*Echinorhinus cookei*). Photo by Craig Racicot / Monterey Bay Aquarium Foundation.

force is focused currently on the distribution and abundance of sixgill and sevengill sharks and their ecological role in Puget Sound. At present researchers are tagging with conventional dart tags, sonic transmitters and shaped visual tags for identification underwater by recreational divers who are encountering the sharks regularly. Researchers are also using DNA analyses for estimates of population structure and organization as well as some very crude estimates of population size. The overall goal of their work is to gain some knowledge about the role these sharks may play in the dynamics of the Puget Sound ecosystem. Plans include designing research to estimate bioenergetic requirements, food preferences and consumption.

The Shark Research Lab at the University of Washington, led by Vincent F. Gallucci, conducts research on sharks with the aim of increasing awareness of sharks and the impacts that humans have upon them, including the effects of pollution and harvesting. Their research methods include field and laboratory experiments, mathematical modeling and statistical analysis.

The Tagging of Pacific Pelagic (TOPP) research project was launched in November 2000. Jointly run by Stanford's Hopkins Marine Lab, the University of California, Santa Cruz's Long Marine Laboratory, NOAA's Pacific Fisheries Ecosystems Lab and the Monterey Bay Aquarium, TOPP also includes team members from several countries. TOPP scientists are tagging individuals from 21 species of marine predators in the eastern Pacific, including salmon shark, great white shark (*Carcharodon carcharias*), shortfin mako (*Isurus oxyrinchus*), blue shark (*Prionace glauca*) and common thresher shark (*Alopias vulpinus*). TOPP scientists are tracking the individuals' movements while recording oceanographic and ecosystem data from their immediate surroundings. Pop-up satellite archival tags are externally attached tags that

During the Lewis and Clark Legacy Expedition to Astoria Canyon and Heceta Bank, Oregon, at a depth of 150 m (492 ft), this bluntnose sixgill shark (*Hexanchus griseus*) glided in front of the ROV camera. *Photo NOAA Fisheries and Pacific Marine Environmental Laboratory.*

contain transmitter-plus-flotation devices. At a pre-set time these tags detach and rise to the surface. These devices then send a summary of the archived data to the researcher via satellites, eliminating the need to recover the tag in order to collect the data recorded. TOPP is also using satellite tags that transmit throughout the track while still attached to the animal.

Another precious source of specimens and data for the ichthyologists that study the sharks are the museums present in the area. The University of Washington Fish Collection (UWFC) of the School of Aquatic and Fishery Sciences is a state-supported facility located on the University of Washington campus in Seattle, Washington. At the UWFC there are over 400 shark specimens. The collection includes adults, juveniles, embryos and the egg cases of numerous species, most of them preserved in ethanol. These specimens have been caught both in the northeastern Pacific Ocean and in other parts of the world. All UWFC material is readily available online. Logging on to www.uw-fishcollection.org the visitor will find a fully searchable portal to all UWFC holdings. Provided with each specimen is a catalog number, taxonomic information, collector, capture date and location, maturity, size, disposition and condition.

At the University of British Columbia Fish Museum in Vancouver, British Columbia, there are about 230 lots of sharks, skates and rays

Replica of a brown catshark (*Apristurus brunneus*) preserved in the Royal British Columbia Museum, Victoria.
Photo by Gavin F. Hanke, courtesy of Royal British Columbia Museum.

(these consist of variable numbers per lot, but typically less than five per lot). UBC Fish Museum specimens are available online at http://www.fishbase.org/museum/SearchFishCollections.php (enter "begins with UBC" in the "Catalogue box," type genus and species names and hit the "Search" button). Provided with each specimen is a catalogue number, taxonomic information, collector, capture date and location, and references.

At the Royal British Columbia Museum (RBCM) in Victoria, British Columbia, there are over 50 shark specimens. These specimens have been caught mostly in British Columbia waters. All RBCM material is available online. Logging on to www.royalbcmuseum.bc.ca the visitor will find a fully searchable portal to all RBCM holdings. Provided with each specimen is a catalogue number, taxonomic information, disposition, capture date and location.

Another way to study sharks is in captivity. Sharks are difficult to keep in captivity: they require large tanks and high water purity, and in these unnatural conditions they consume a very small amount

Leopard sharks (*Triakis semifasciata*) at the Oregon Coast Aquarium. *Photo by Cindy Hanson, courtesy of Oregon Coast Aquarium.*

of food. They can also stop feeding for many weeks or months and sometimes die. For these reasons and because of other problems related to their physiological needs, many shark species, especially those of large size and having pelagic habits, are rarely kept in aquaria. The observation of captive specimens permits us to study their swimming, reproduction and sensorial abilities; the study of shark behavior under these conditions has often been criticized because the behavior of a specimen forced to live in a tank cannot be considered normal and it cannot be assumed to be equal or even similar to that of a free specimen.

Aquaria in the area include the Oregon Coast Aquarium in Newport, Oregon; Seattle Aquarium in Seattle, Washington; Point Defiance Zoo & Aquarium in Tacoma, Washington; Vancouver Aquarium in Vancouver, British Columbia; and the Alaska SeaLife Center in Seward, Alaska. The Oregon Coast Aquarium hosts four species of sharks living in Oregon waters: broadnose sevengill shark (*Notorynchus cepedianus*), piked dogfish, tope shark (*Galeorhinus galeus*) and leopard shark (*Triakis semifasciata*), while Point Defiance Zoo & Aquarium and Vancouver Aquarium have only tropical species.

RESEARCH INSTITUTES

Several research programs and occasional studies are conducted in the area by ichthyologists and biologists working in marine biology institutes, natural history museums and universities. Provided here is a list of the institutes where research on sharks in the Pacific Northwest is currently carried out, including contact addresses.

Alaska Department of Fish and Game
P.O. Box 115525, 1255 West 8th Street, Juneau, Alaska 99811-5526 USA
E-mail: lee_hulbert@fishgame.state.ak.us
Website: http://www.adfg.state.ak.us/

Conservation Science Institute
P.O. Box 7924, Santa Cruz, California 95061 USA
E-mail: bruce.wright@conservationinstitute.org
Website: http://www.conservationinstitute.org

Global Shark Attack File

P.O. Box 40, Princeton, New Jersey 08540 USA
E-mail: info@sharkattackfile.net
Website: www.sharkattackfile.net

NOAA Fisheries Auke Bay Laboratory

11305 Glacier Highway, Juneau, Alaska 99801 USA
E-mail: lee_hulbert@fishgame.state.ak.us
Website: http://www.afsc.noaa.gov/

NOAA's National Marine Fisheries Service, Northwest Regional Office

7600 Sand Point Way NE, Seattle, Washington 98115-0070 USA
E-mail: Bob.Lohn@noaa.gov
Website: http://www.nwr.noaa.gov/

Oregon Coast Aquarium

2820 SE Ferry Slip Road, Newport, Oregon 97365 USA
E-mail: info@aquarium.org
Website: http://www.aquarium.org

Point Defiance Zoo & Aquarium

5400 N. Pearl St., Tacoma, Washington 98407 USA
E-mail: pdzacomments@tacomaparks.com
Website: http://www.pdza.org

ReefQuest Centre for Shark Research

P.O. Box 48561, 595 Burrard Street, Vancouver, British Columbia V7X 1A3
  Canada
E-mail: r.aidan.martin@elasmo-research.org
Website: http://www.elasmo-research.org

School of Fisheries and Ocean Sciences, University of Alaska Fairbanks

11120 Glacier HWY, Juneau, Alaska 99801 USA
E-mail: gordon.kruse@uaf.edu
Website: http://www.sfos.uaf.edu/

Seattle Aquarium

1483 Alaskan Way, Seattle, Washington 98101 USA
E-mail: aquarium.programs@seattle.gov
Website: http://www.seattleaquarium.org

Shark Research Committee
P.O. Box 3483, Van Nuys, California 91407 USA
E-mail: SharkResearch@aol.com
Website: http://www.sharkresearchcommittee.com

Stanford University Hopkins Marine Station
Oceanview Boulevard, Pacific Grove, California 93950-3094 USA
E-mail: information@marine.stanford.edu
Website: http://www-marine.stanford.edu/

University of Alberta Department of Biological Sciences
CW 405, Biological Sciences Centre, Edmonton, Alberta T6G 2E9 Canada
E-mail: jbruner@gpu.srv.ualberta.ca
Website: http://www.biology.ualberta.ca/

University of British Columbia Department of Zoology
#2370-6270 University Blvd., Vancouver, British Columbia V6T 1Z4 Canada
E-mail: shadwick@zoology.ubc.ca
Website: http://www.zoology.ubc.ca/

University of Washington Shark Research Lab
School of Aquatic and Fishery Sciences, 1122 NE Boat St., Seattle, Washington 98105 USA
E-mail: vgallucc@u.washington.edu
Website: http://www.fish.washington.edu/research/sharks

Washington Department of Fish and Wildlife
Natural Resources Building, 1111 Washington St. SE, Olympia, Washington 98501 USA
E-mail: webmaster@dfw.wa.gov
Website: http://wdfw.wa.gov

The prickly shark (*Echinorhinus cookei*) is especially difficult to study, since it is an uncommon species and favors deep waters. *Painting by Alessandro De Maddalena.*

REPORTING ENCOUNTERS

Everyone can help in the research on sharks located in the waters of the Pacific Northwest. Reporting the captures and sightings of sharks is the best way to do it. The data that is collected with your help will be archived for future studies. Note that information on the capture and sighting of *all* shark species is considered interesting, not just information concerning the larger species.

To help with this data collection, please see the form on the next page. The information in the form must be as accurate and complete as possible; however, do not hesitate to send incomplete forms. For those who go sport fishing and capture a shark, we strongly recommend you set the animal free after capture. In this way, you can help avoid the unnecessary killing of these wonderful animals, which are already in alarming decline. Obviously, in this case, it will not be important if the form is not completely filled out.

We need to clarify some points in order to make your contribution as useful as possible. We strongly suggest that you measure the total length of the shark in a straight line from the snout to the tip of the upper lobe of the caudal fin. If you do not have the means to accurately measure the specimen, you will need to specify that the

Report of sightings or captures of sharks in the Pacific Northwest

Shark species:

On which characteristics do you recognize the species?

Type of record (capture, underwater encounter, sighting or attack):

Date:

Time:

Location (if possible, indicate the exact position):

Position (latitude and longitude):

Sea depth:

Distance from the coast:

Weather:

State of the sea:

Activity of the observer at the time of the encounter:

Total length:

Weight (specify if whole or gutted):

Sex:

Stomach contents:

Comments on the behavior of the specimen:

If it's a pregnant female add:

        Number of embryos:

        Total length of embryos:

        Weight of embryos:

        Sex of embryos:

Presence of other animals in the immediate area:

Other details and comments:

Name of the eyewitness / fisherman / diver:

Contact information

        Name:

        Address:

        Telephone:

        E-mail:

Enclose a photo of the specimen.

Do you authorize the publication of these pictures and/or data?

        Please fill in this form and return to:
        Shark Research Committee, P.O. Box 3483, Van Nuys, CA 91407 USA
        E-mail: SharkResearch@aol.com

reported measure is an estimate.

The weight is considered less important, although it has to be taken on the whole specimen; otherwise, you will need to state if the specimen has been gutted, beheaded, finned or other. If you can't weigh the specimen, you will need to state that the reported weight is an estimate.

Remember that the sex of the specimen is easily recognizable by observing the underside of the shark at the level of the pelvic fins (the pair of fins located in the pelvic region), where males have two claspers (copulatory organs) in the shape of cylindrical appendages.

Try to take a photo of the shark: it will be very useful both for identification of the species and for our archives. When you shoot a photo of the shark, try to include the whole specimen, from its side; additional photos of details, especially the underside of the head and the teeth, are also suggested.

Chapter 3

Classification
and Species
Identification

CLASSIFICATION

Listed below are the 18 shark species reported in the waters of the Pacific Northwest. These are classified into 5 orders, 10 families and 14 genera. The list includes even the very rare species, but does not include the species that lack at least one confirmed record and for which only anecdotal accounts exist.

ORDER HEXANCHIFORMES

FAMILY HEXANCHIDAE
Genus Hexanchus
Hexanchus griseus — Bluntnose sixgill shark

Genus Notorynchus
Notorynchus cepedianus — Broadnose sevengill shark

ORDER SQUALIFORMES

FAMILY ECHINORHINIDAE
Genus Echinorhinus
Echinorhinus cookei — Prickly shark

FAMILY SQUALIDAE
Genus Squalus
Squalus acanthias — Piked dogfish or spiny dogfish

FAMILY SOMNIOSIDAE
Genus Somniosus
Somniosus pacificus — Pacific sleeper shark

ORDER SQUATINIFORMES

FAMILY SQUATINIDAE
Genus Squatina
Squatina californica — Pacific angelshark

ORDER LAMNIFORMES

FAMILY ALOPIIDAE
Genus Alopias
Alopias vulpinus — Common thresher shark

Opposite inset: Piked dogfish or spiny dogfish (*Squalus acanthias*). Photo by Bernie Hanby.

FAMILY CETORHINIDAE
Genus Cetorhinus
> *Cetorhinus maximus* — Basking shark

FAMILY LAMNIDAE
Genus Carcharodon
> *Carcharodon carcharias* — Great white shark

Genus Isurus
> *Isurus oxyrinchus* — Shortfin mako

Genus Lamna
> *Lamna ditropis* — Salmon shark

ORDER CARCHARHINIFORMES

FAMILY SCYLIORHINIDAE
Genus Apristurus
> *Apristurus brunneus* — Brown catshark
> *Apristurus kampae* — Longnose catshark

Genus Parmaturus
> *Parmaturus xaniurus* — Filetail catshark

FAMILY TRIAKIDAE
Genus Galeorhinus
> *Galeorhinus galeus* — Tope shark

Genus Mustelus
> *Mustelus henlei* — Brown smoothhound

Genus Triakis
> *Triakis semifasciata* — Leopard shark

FAMILY CARCHARHINIDAE
Genus Prionace
> *Prionace glauca* — Blue shark

INTRODUCTION TO SPECIES IDENTIFICATION

Some species inhabiting the waters of the Pacific Northwest, such as the common thresher (*Alopias vulpinus*) and the basking shark (*Cetorhinus maximus*), are very easy to identify even by a non-specialist.

But for other species the identification is not so simple. Moreover, the morphology of a shark can show high variability within each species, depending on age.

What do we need to look for when identifying a shark? It is necessary to look at the size (remembering that it is possible to encounter a juvenile); body shape; length and shape of snout; absence or presence and size of spiracles; size and color of eyes; and number, size and position of gill slits. In some cases teeth can be prominent and highly visible exteriorly, and their shape evident. The shape and position of fins is one of the most important diagnostic characteristics, and in some species a dorsal fin or the anal fin can be absent. Even coloration can help in species identification, especially when the shark shows a particular pattern, bearing in mind that juveniles can sometimes show differences in coloration, particularly in tips and posterior margins of fins, which often can be lighter or darker than in adults. Dead specimens lose the brightness of color that they had while alive. If the specimen that has to be identified is

A piked dogfish (*Squalus acanthias*). While this species is easy to identify, the exact identification of other shark species can be harder if the animal is only observed from above, as when seen from a boat. *Photo by Gordon McFarlane.*

Broadnose sevengill sharks (*Notorynchus cepedianus*). The 7 pairs of gill slits make them unmistakable. *Photo by Gianluca Cugini.*

dead, it may be possible to look closely at both the shape and number of teeth in order to have an additional tool for identification through its dental formula.

KEY TO THE SPECIES

In order to easily identify the species of a given animal group, scientific books often include keys to identification: the reader has to reply to a series of questions related to the external morphology of the specimen that needs to be identified, and each reply is followed by another step that takes the reader closer to identification. Unfortunately, the keys are often too long and based on characteristics not easily observable and not infrequently result in uncertain identification. We tried to avoid this problem by preparing a key to identification that is the simpliest possible.

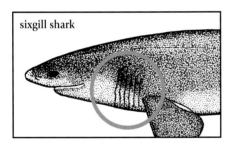

sixgill shark

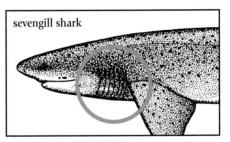

sevengill shark

1a) 5 pairs of gill slits: go to Number 2
1b) 6 pairs of gill slits: **sixgill shark** (*Hexanchus griseus*)
1c) 7 pairs of gill slits: **broadnose sevengill shark** (*Notorynchus cepedianus*)

2a) anal fin absent: go to Number 3
2b) anal fin present go to Number 6

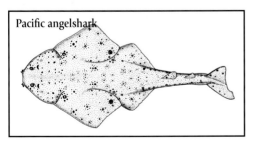

Pacific angelshark

3a) body ray-like, strongly dorso-ventrally flattened: **pacific angelshark** (*Squatina californica*)
3b) body not ray-like: go to Number 4

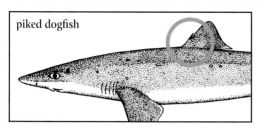

4a) spines present on both dorsal fins: **piked dogfish or spiny dogfish** (*Squalus acanthias*)

4b) spines absent on both dorsal fins: go to Number 5

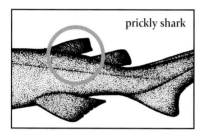

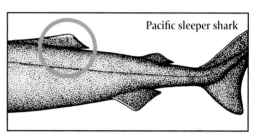

5a) origin of the first dorsal fin over pelvic fins: **prickly shark** (*Echinorhinus cookei*)

5b) origin of the first dorsal fin well in front of pelvic fins: **Pacific sleeper shark** (*Somniosus pacificus*)

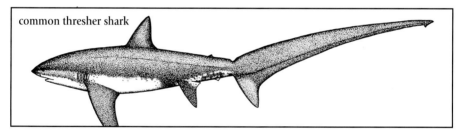

6a) upper lobe of caudal fin as long as the rest of the shark: **common thresher shark** (*Alopias vulpinus*)

6b) upper lobe of caudal fin much shorter than the rest of the shark: go to Number 7

7a) gill slits very long: go to Number 8

7b) gill slits short: go to Number 11

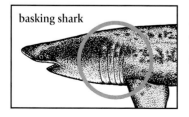

8a) gill slits almost completely encircling the head: **basking shark** (*Cetorhinus maximus*)

8b) gill slits not encircling the head: go to Number 9

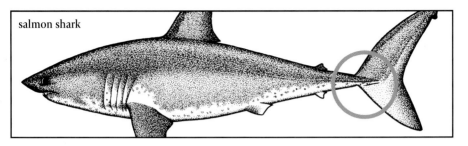

salmon shark

9a) two pairs of caudal keels: **salmon shark** (*Lamna ditropis*)
9b) one pair of caudal keels: go to Number 10

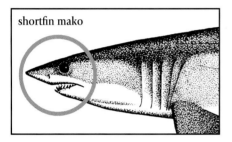

shortfin mako

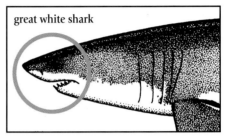

great white shark

10a) snout narrow; teeth long, narrow and with cutting edges: **shortfin mako** (*Isurus oxyrinchus*)
10b) snout wide; teeth triangular with serrated edges: **great white shark** (*Carcharodon carcharias*)

11a) origin of the first dorsal fin over pelvic fins: go to Number 12
11b) origin of the first dorsal fin well in front of pelvic fins: go to Number 14

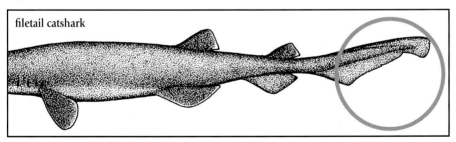

filetail catshark

12a) anterior margin of upper caudal lobe with a prominent row of enlarged dermal denticles: **filetail catshark** (*Parmaturus xaniurus*)
12b) anterior margin of upper caudal lobe without enlarged dermal denticles: go to Number 13

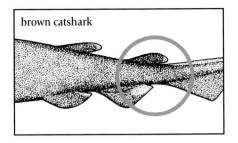 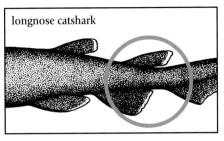

13a) upper labial folds longer than lower; anal fin nearly reaching the base of the caudal fin: **brown catshark** (*Apristurus brunneus*)

13b) lower labial folds longer than upper; anal fin doesn't reach the base of the caudal fin: **longnose catshark** (*Apristurus kampae*)

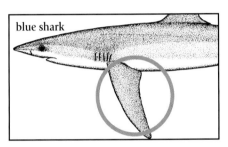

14a) spiracles absent; pectoral fins very long: **blue shark** (*Prionace glauca*)

14b) spiracles present; pectoral fins short: go to Number 15

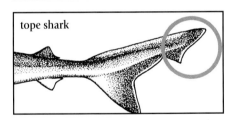

15a) terminal lobe of caudal fin huge; second dorsal fin small: **tope shark** (*Galeorhinus galeus*) or soupfin shark

15b) terminal lobe of caudal fin moderately large; second dorsal fin large: go to Number 16

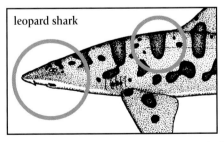 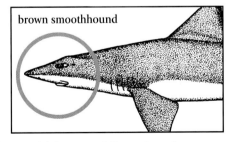

16a) snout short; coloration with large black to grayish brown saddle marks and spots: **leopard shark** (*Triakis semifasciata*)

16b) snout long; coloration uniform brown or gray: **brown smoothhound** (*Mustelus henlei*)

Chapter 4

Species Profiles

ABOUT THIS SECTION

This part of the book gives detailed and fully updated information on all the shark species recorded in the waters of the Pacific Northwest. For each species we include the following information and illustrations.

Common name, Latin name (followed by the name of the naturalist who first described the species and the year in which the description was published), illustrations (drawings of lateral view, ventral view of the head, upper and lower teeth, ventral view of the pectoral fin, and photo), classification (order, family, genus), morphology, coloration, teeth shape, dental formula (teeth in the right side of the upper jaw – teeth in the left side of the upper jaw / teeth in the right side of the lower jaw – teeth in the left side of the lower jaw), maximum size (usually the total length, in a straight line from the snout to the tip of the upper lobe of the caudal fin), size at birth (total length), size at maturity (total length; male and female), embryonic development (oviparous, aplacental viviparous, placental viviparous), gestation, litter size (minimum and maximum), maximum age, diet (usually as taxonomic classes), habitat (sea region and depth range), distribution in the area, distribution in the rest of the world, behavior, threat to humans (not dangerous, potentially dangerous, dangerous, highly dangerous).

Opposite inset: A basking shark (Cetorhinus maximus). Photo by Chris Gotschalk.

Bluntnose sixgill shark

Hexanchus griseus Bonnaterre, 1788

Classification: order Hexanchiformes, family Hexanchidae, genus *Hexanchus*.

Morphology: 6 pairs of long gill slits, all located anteriorly to the pectoral fin anterior margin. The first gill slits are longer than the following. A unique dorsal fin, located backward, with its origin over the posterior part of the pelvic fins, moderately large. Pectoral fins moderately long but wide. Caudal fin upper lobe long to very long, lower short. Caudal peduncle short, its length equal or slightly longer than the dorsal fin base. Body massive, head wide and rounded in dorso-ventral view. Mouth very wide and long. Eyes relatively large. Spiracles small.

Coloration: dorsal surfaces light gray, dark gray, black, brownish or yellow ochre, and lighter along the lateral line; ventral surfaces

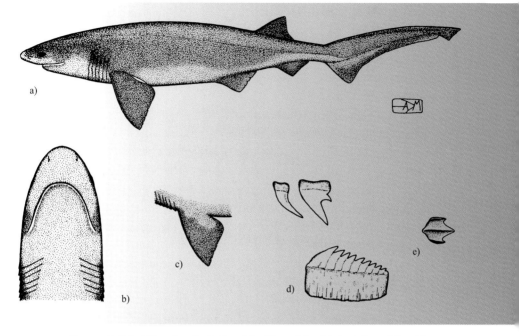

Bluntnose sixgill shark (*Hexanchus griseus*): a) lateral view, b) ventral view of the head, c) ventral view of the pectoral fin, d) upper and lower teeth, e) placoid scale. *Drawings by Alessandro De Maddalena.*

lighter than the dorsal surfaces or even whitish, except the gill slits region, which shows an irregular dark coloration similar to that of the dorsal surfaces. Sometimes the fin posterior margins are white, and there is a white area at the pectoral fin axil. The pectoral fin ventral surface has the same dark coloration as the dorsal surface, except at the base, which is whitish gray. Eyes fluorescent green. Coloration lighter in juveniles; newborns have the anterior edges of fins whitish.

Teeth shape: upper teeth narrow and pointed with one cusp, and with or without 1–3 cusplets depending on the tooth position; lower teeth much larger, comblike, with up to 11 cusplets.

Dental formula: 9 to 10 – 9 to 10 / 6 – 1 – 6.

Maximum size: at least 482 cm (190 in), but it is estimated to pass 500 cm (197 in).

Size at birth: 56–70 cm (22–28 in).

Size at maturity: male: 320–350 cm (126–138 in); female: 396 cm (156 in).

Embryonic development: aplacental viviparous.

Gestation: unknown.

Litter size: 22–108 young.

Maximum age: unknown.

Diet: cartilaginous fishes, bony fishes, cephalopods, gastropods, crustaceans, marine mammals, sea urchins, carcasses.

Habitat: mainly in deep waters, benthic, on continental and insular shelves and upper slopes, at depths ranging from 0 to at least 2,500 m (8,200 ft). Juveniles occur in shallower waters than adults.

Distribution in the area: all Oregon, Washington and British Columbia waters; in Alaska its range extends northward to Aleutian Islands.

Distribution in the rest of the world: Atlantic, Pacific and Indian Oceans.

Behavior: slow, nocturnal, occur singly or in pairs, can approach divers closely (without showing any aggressive behavior), usually show little resistance even when hooked.

Threat to humans: not dangerous.

Notes: Bluntnose sixgill sharks are common in the Pacific Northwest. Flora Islets in the Strait of Georgia, British Columbia, is a bluntnose sixgill shark diving hotspot. The sharks are present during the summer months between April and September; their frequency increases in June and reaches a peak between mid-June and mid-July. The optimum depth for sightings seems to be in the 18 to 30 m (60–100 ft) range. Bluntnose sixgill shark frequency is highest in the afternoon. This shallow-water activity is not related to either reproduction or feeding and its purpose remains unclear. Divers encounter sixgill sharks off Saanich Inlet and Barkley Sound, British Columbia, and the San Juan Islands and Hood Canal,

A bluntnose sixgill shark (*Hexanchus griseus*) photographed off Hornby Island in the Strait of Georgia. *Photo by Phil Edgell.*

Washington. A longline fishery targeting sixgill sharks was conducted in Puget Sound, Washington, in the 1980s, and a small recreational fishery exists in Puget Sound. These sharks are occasionally taken incidentally with trawl or longline gear in Oregon. Attempts have been made to commence a fishery for bluntnose sixgill sharks in British Columbia, but these efforts were unsuccessful because of concerns over the sustainability of such a fishery given insufficient knowledge about the resource.

Broadnose sevengill shark

Notorynchus cepedianus Peron, 1807

Classification: order Hexanchiformes, family Hexanchidae, genus *Notorynchus*.

Morphology: 7 pairs of long gill slits, all located anteriorly to the pectoral fin anterior margin. A unique dorsal fin, located backward, with its origin over the posterior part of the pelvic fins, moderately large. Pectoral fins moderately long but wide. Caudal fin upper lobe long to very long, lower short. Body massive, head wide and rounded in dorso-ventral view. Mouth very wide and long. Eyes relatively large. Spiracles small.

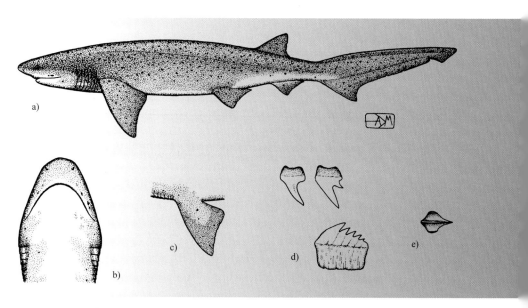

Broadnose sevengill shark (*Notorynchus cepedianus*): a) lateral view, b) ventral view of the head, c) ventral view of the pectoral fin, d) upper and lower teeth, e) placoid scale. *Drawings by Alessandro De Maddalena.*

Coloration: dorsal surfaces gray to reddish brown or olive brown with dark spots; off-white ventral surfaces, except the gill slits region, which shows an irregular dark coloration similar to that of the dorsal surfaces. Sometimes the fin posterior margins are white. A white area at the pectoral fin axil. The pectoral fin ventral surface is whitish gray. White spots occasionally found on back and sides are attributable to a fungus. This shark may be able to alter its coloration slightly. Rare cases of albino specimens exist.

Broadnose sevengill shark (*Notorynchus cepedianus*). *Photo by Cindy Hanson, courtesy of Oregon Coast Aquarium.*

Teeth shape: upper teeth narrow and pointed with one cusp and with or without 1–2 cusplets depending on the tooth position; lower teeth much larger, comblike, with up to 6 cusplets.

Dental formula: 7 – 1 – 7 / 6 – 1 – 6.

Maximum size: at least 290 cm (114 in) and probably over 300 cm (118 in).

Size at birth: 35–45 cm (14–18 in).

Size at maturity: male: 150–180 cm (59–71 in); female: 192–208 cm (75–82 in).

Embryonic development: aplacental viviparous.

Gestation: unknown.

Litter size: up to 83 young.

Maximum age: unknown.

Diet: cartilaginous fishes, bony fishes, marine mammals, carcasses.

Habitat: benthic, on continental shelves, at depths ranging from 0 to at least 136 m (446 ft); pregnant females can give birth in shallow waters.

Distribution in the area: all Oregon, Washington and British Columbia waters; in Alaska its range extends northward to Alexander Archipelago.

Distribution in the rest of the world: Atlantic, Pacific and Indian Oceans.

Behavior: active, uses stealth to ambush prey, hunts cooperatively in packs to subdue large prey, usually shows great resistance when hooked.

Threat to humans: potentially dangerous.

Notes: Broadnose sevengill sharks are relatively common in estuaries on the coast of Washington, where they are seasonally present during the summer months. In the winter, broadnose sevengill sharks are found off Oregon and in Puget Sound, Washington. In Alaska there are reports of large broadnose sevengill sharks attacking harbor seals; perhaps they hunt cooperatively in packs to kill their prey. Broadnose sevengill sharks are occasionally caught as bycatch in Oregon drift gillnet fisheries for swordfish and sharks. They are also caught by sport fishers. In the 1930s and 1940s these sharks were fished for their vitamin A-rich liver until the vitamin was synthesized.

Prickly shark

Echinorhinus cookei Pietschmann, 1928

Classification: order Squaliformes, family Echinorhinidae, genus *Echinorhinus*.

Morphology: no anal fin. Dorsal fins located backwards, the origin of the first dorsal over pelvic fins. First dorsal fin about as large as the second dorsal. Pelvic fins large. Pectoral fins short. Caudal fin upper lobe large, lower lobe short. Caudal fin lacking posterior notch. Fin posterior margins frayed. Body massive and stout. Caudal peduncle large. Dermal denticles large (diameter up to 0.4 cm/0.15 in) and pointed. Eyes large. Nostrils wide. Spiracles small. 5 pairs of relatively small gill slits, all located anteriorly to pectoral fin origin, the first gill slits shorter than the following.

Coloration: dorsal surfaces gray-brown; ventral surfaces similar, but

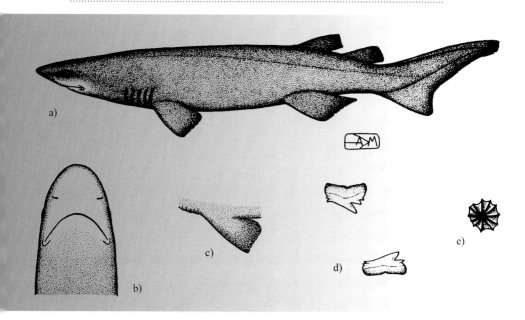

Prickly shark (*Echinorhinus cookei*): a) lateral view, b) ventral view of the head, c) ventral view of the pectoral fin, d) upper and lower teeth, e) placoid scale. *Drawings by Alessandro De Maddalena.*

the underside of the head is lighter or white. Fins have black posterior margins.

Teeth shape: upper teeth small, with a low oblique cusp and 2–4 cusplets; lower teeth similar.

Dental formula: 10 to 12 – 10 to 12 / 11 to 14 – 11 to 14.

Maximum size: 400 cm (157 in).

Size at birth: 35–45 cm (14–18 in).

Size at maturity: male: 240 cm (94.5 in); female: 254–299 cm (100–118 in).

Embryonic development: aplacental viviparous.

Gestation: unknown.

Litter size: up to 114.

Maximum age: unknown.

Diet: sharks, bony fishes, cephalopods, crustaceans.

Habitat: benthic, mainly in deep waters, on continental and insular shelves and upper slopes, at depths ranging from 11 to at least 650 m (36–2,132 ft).

Distribution in the area: Oregon; its range extends northward to Moolach Beach.

Distribution in the rest of the world: Pacific Ocean.

Behavior: occur singly or in groups, probably feed by suctioning to inhale prey.

Threat to humans: not dangerous.

Notes: Prickly sharks are very rare in Oregon waters. These sharks periodically congregate in groups over sandy bottoms. Prickly sharks were occasionally caught as bycatch in Oregon drift gillnet fisheries for swordfish and sharks. Because of the depth at which this species is typically found, knowledge is extremely limited concerning the life history of these large sharks.

Piked dogfish or spiny dogfish

Squalus acanthias Smith & Radcliffe, 1912

Classification: order Squaliformes, family Squalidae, genus *Squalus*.

Morphology: no anal fin. Fin spines on both dorsal fins, the first spine short, the second spine slightly longer. First dorsal fin moderately large, second dorsal smaller; first dorsal fin origin posterior to pectoral fin free rear tip. Pectoral fins moderately wide. No caudal fin subterminal notch. Caudal fin upper lobe moderately long, lower lobe short. Small caudal keels. Snout long. Mouth almost straight in ventral view. Long labial folds. Eyes large. Spiracles large. 5 pairs of short gill slits, all located anteriorly to the pectoral fin origin.

Coloration: dorsal surfaces bluish gray or brown with some small white spots; ventral surfaces white. Pectoral, pelvic, caudal fins with posterior margin light; first dorsal fin apex dark. The pectoral fin ventral surface is gray like the dorsal surface, faded in the basal part and with the posterior margin white. In the adult the white spots can be partially faded and perhaps sometimes disappear.

Teeth shape: upper teeth with one cusp, small, oblique, almost horizontal, with cutting edges, the teeth are interlocked forming a sort of cutting wall; lower teeth similar.

Dental formula: 12 to 14 – 12 to 14 / 11 to 12 – 11 to 12.

Maximum size: 160 cm (63 in).

Size at birth: 20–33 cm (8–13 in).

Size at maturity: male: 56–80 cm (22–31.5 in); female: 60–100 cm (24–39 in).

Embryonic development: aplacental viviparous.

Gestation: 18–24 months.

Litter size: 1–20 young.

Maximum age: at least 40 years and possibly up to 100 years.

Diet: bony fishes, cartilaginous fishes, cephalopods, gastropods, crustaceans, polichetes, sea cucumbers, ctenophores, hydrozoans, jellyfishes.

Habitat: pelagic, on continental and insular shelves and upper slopes, at depths ranging from 0 to at least 1,236 m (4,055 ft). Males occur in shallower waters than females; pregnant females can give birth in shallow waters.

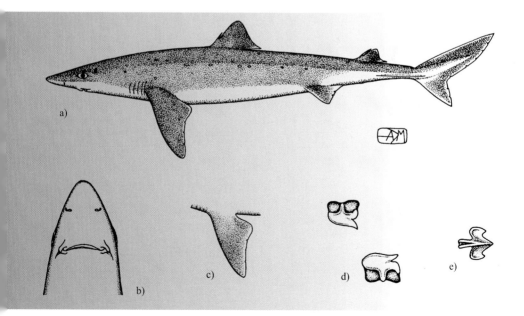

Piked dogfish (*Squalus acanthias*): a) lateral view, b) ventral view of the head, c) ventral view of the pectoral fin, d) upper and lower teeth, e) placoid scale. *Drawings by Alessandro De Maddalena.*

Distribution in the area: all Oregon, Washington and British Columbia waters; in Alaska its range extends northward to Bering Sea.

Distribution in the rest of the world: Atlantic and Pacific Oceans.

Behavior: active, occur singly or in enormous groups, migratory, timid, can segregate by sex and size, use the dorsal fin spines as a defensive weapon.

Threat to humans: not dangerous.

Notes: Piked dogfish are common in the Pacific Northwest, more common off Oregon, Washington and British Columbia than in the Gulf of Alaska. Prehistoric records confirm the common use of this shark by North American natives in the region since about 4000–4600 BP. Piked dogfish became the object of an important targeted fishery off British Columbia in the 1940s for their vitamin A-rich livers. This fishery reduced their populations and then declined. An intense fishery was re-instituted in the 1970s. The piked

A piked dogfish
(*Squalus
acanthias*)
photographed
off Fox Island,
Washington.
*Photo by Greg
Amptman.*

dogfish fishery also occurs in Puget Sound, Washington, and to a lesser extent off Oregon. Piked dogfish are also taken as part of the recreational fishery. From 1978 to 1988, 71,000 piked dogfish were tagged off British Columbia. Generally, tagged sharks were recaptured close to their release site, however, extensive migrations did occur: piked dogfish from British Columbia were recaptured off California, Alaska and Japan. In British Columbia and Washington waters there are both largely resident and seasonally migrating groups. Quadra Island, British Columbia, is a piked dogfish diving hotspot, where thousands of these sharks accumulate each summer.

Pacific sleeper shark

Somniosus pacificus Bigelow & Schroeder, 1944

Classification: order Squaliformes, family Somniosidae, genus *Somniosus*.

Morphology: cylindrical body. No anal fin. Pectoral fins short. Dorsal fins low, the first dorsal slightly larger than second dorsal, its origin posterior to the pectoral fin free rear tip. Caudal fin upper lobe moderately long, lower lobe almost as large as the upper lobe. Snout rounded. Mouth almost straight in ventral view; lower labial folds long. Spiracles small. 5 pairs of short gill slits, all located anteriorly to the pectoral fin origin and in a lower position.

Coloration: dorsal surfaces gray to blackish brown, often with darker mottling; ventral surfaces similar.

Teeth shape: upper teeth with smooth edges and having one small vertical cusp; lower teeth larger, with one cusp, oblique, with smooth edges.

Dental formula: 26 – 1 – 26 / 26 – 1 – 26.

Maximum size: at least 430 cm (169 in) and probably up to 700 cm (275 in).

Size at birth: about 65 cm (25 in).

Size at maturity: male: about 400 cm (157 in); female: about 370 cm (146 in).

Embryonic development: aplacental viviparous.

Gestation: unknown.

Litter size: unknown.

Maximum age: unknown.

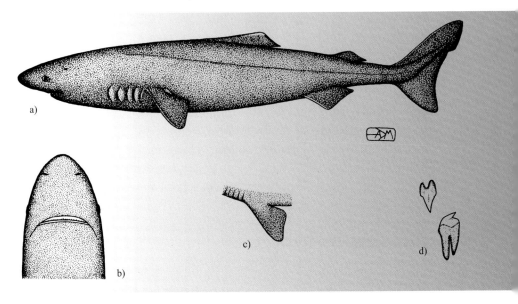

Pacific sleeper shark (*Somniosus pacificus*): a) lateral view, b) ventral view of the head, c) ventral view of the pectoral fin, d) upper and lower teeth. *Drawings by Alessandro De Maddalena.*

Diet: bony fishes, cephalopods, crustaceans, marine mammals, carcasses.

Habitat: mainly benthic, in deep waters, on outer continental shelves and upper slopes, at depths ranging from 200 to at least 1,975 m (656–6,480 ft).

Distribution in the area: all Oregon, Washington and British Columbia waters; in Alaska its range extends northward to Chukchi Sea.

Distribution in the rest of the world: Pacific Ocean.

Behavior: it may be able to capture fast-swimming prey by lying in wait and ambushing it, and probably feeds by suctioning to inhale its prey.

Threat to humans: not dangerous.

Notes: Pacific sleeper sharks are common in the Pacific Northwest and their abundance has significantly increased in the Gulf of Alaska during the 1990s. In the Gulf of Alaska, they make extensive and continuous vertical movements: the sharks travel below the photic zone during the day and approach the surface at night. These large sharks appear to employ a stealth and ambush hunting strategy that includes vertical oscillations to search for prey, and cryptic coloration and cover of darkness to avoid detection. In the Gulf of

Pacific sleeper
shark *(Somniosus
pacificus)*. *Photo
(c) 2004 MBARI.*

Alaska, Pacific sleeper sharks are commonly found near Steller sea lion rookeries. In Alaskan waters, they feed on bony fish, cephalopods and marine mammals. Some Pacific sleeper sharks captured in Prince William Sound, Alaska, were infected with the parasitic copepod *Ommatokoita elongata*, which were attached to the corneas of the sharks' eyes. This parasite can reach lengths up to 8 cm (3 in). These infections can lead to severe vision impairment, but some researchers think that these infections do not significantly debilitate hosts because they probably do not need to rely on acute vision for their survival. This whitish yellow, possibly luminescent, parasite is speculated to lure prey to the Pacific sleeper shark under a mutualistic relationship.

Pacific angelshark
Squatina californica Ayres, 1859

Classification: order Squatiniformes, family Squatinidae, genus *Squatina*.

Morphology: body ray-like: strongly dorso-ventrally flattened, with very wide head and very wide pectoral and pelvic fins. No anal fin. Dorsal fins backwards. Caudal fin lower lobe larger than upper lobe. Caudal keels. Mouth terminal and very wide. Eyes located on dorsal surface of the head. Nasal barbels conical and anterior nasal flaps weakly fringed. Large spiracles. 5 pairs of gill slits, close together, all located anteriorly to the pectoral fin origin, not visible when the shark rests on the sea bottom.

Coloration: dorsal surfaces gray to reddish brown with numerous

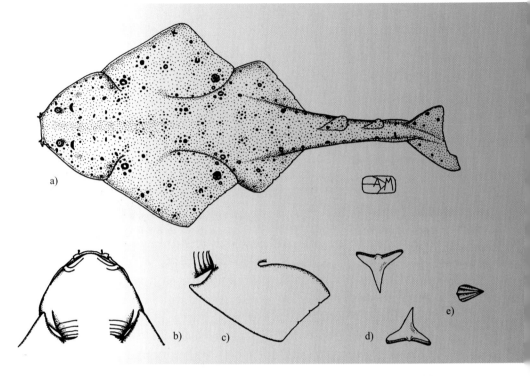

Pacific angelshark (*Squatina californica*): a) dorsal view, b) ventral view of the head, c) ventral view of the pectoral fin, d) upper and lower teeth, e) placoid scale. *Drawings by Alessandro De Maddalena.*

small darker spots, some of them forming slight rings; ventral surfaces white.

Teeth shape: upper teeth with one cusp, small and pointed; lower teeth similar.

Dental formula: 7 to 9 – 7 to 9 / 7 to 10 – 7 to 10.

Maximum size: 152 cm (60 in).

Size at birth: 21–26 cm (8–10 in).

Size at maturity: male: about 100 cm (39 in); female: about 100–120 cm (39–47 in).

Embryonic development: aplacental viviparous.

Gestation: 10 months.

Litter size: 1–13 young.

Maximum age: 35 years.

Diet: bony fishes, cephalopods.

Habitat: benthic, on continental shelves and upper slopes, at depths ranging from 0 to at least 183 m (600 ft).

Distribution in the area: all Oregon, Washington and British Columbia waters; in Alaska its range extends northward to Alexander Archipelago.

Distribution in the rest of the world: eastern Pacific Ocean.

Behavior: torpid and slow, nocturnal, occurs singly, timid, lies buried in the sand of the sea floor and strikes at high speed to capture its prey thanks to its highly protrusible jaws.

Threat to humans: not dangerous.

Notes: It is unusual to encounter Pacific angelsharks in Pacific Northwest waters. Pacific angelsharks occur in several discrete isolated populations. Some of these populations are so distinct from each other that some researchers think that they may in fact represent an entirely different species. Further research is needed to clarify exactly how these populations are interrelated. Pacific angelsharks are occasionally caught as bycatch in Oregon drift gillnet fisheries for swordfish and sharks. These sharks are also taken by recreational anglers.

Pacific angelshark (*Squatina californica*). *Photo by Tony Chess.*

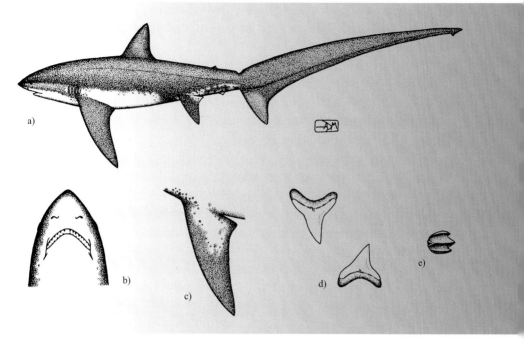

Common thresher shark (*Alopias vulpinus*): a) lateral view, b) ventral view of the head, c) ventral view of the pectoral fin, d) upper and lower teeth, e) placoid scale. *Drawings by Alessandro De Maddalena.*

Common thresher shark

Alopias vulpinus Bonnaterre, 1788

Classification: order Lamniformes, family Alopiidae, genus *Alopias*.

Morphology: caudal fin upper lobe extremely long, about as long as the rest of the body, lower lobe relatively short. Eyes large, but not extending up to the dorsal surface of the head. Dorsal part pronounced. Snout conical. Pectoral and pelvic fins long. First dorsal fin large, its origin posterior to pectoral fin free rear tip. Second dorsal and anal fins very small. Caudal peduncle large. Mouth relatively small. Spiracles very small. 5 pairs of short gill slits, the 4th and 5th located over the pectoral fin base.

Coloration: dorsal surfaces dark bluish gray, with metallic reflections on the sides; ventral surfaces white except on the pelvic region and caudal peduncle where the dark coloration extends, forming an irregular indented pattern with patches and small spots. Boundary separating dorsal from ventral coloration sharp on the head. The pectoral fin ventral surface has extended dark coloration like

the dorsal surface and with indented margins forming irregular patches and a white V-shaped area at the basal part.

Teeth shape: upper teeth with one cusp, pointed and oblique, with cutting edges; lower teeth similar.

Dental formula: 19 to 26 – 0 to 1 – 19 to 26 / 21 to 24 – 0 to 1 – 21 to 24.

Maximum size: at least 636 cm (250 in).

Size at birth: 114–155 cm (45–61 in).

Size at maturity: male: 320–333 cm (126–131 in); female: 375–420 cm (148–165 in).

Embryonic development: aplacental viviparous (embryos nourished by oophagy).

Gestation: 9 months.

Litter size: 2–7 young.

Maximum age: at least 19 years.

Diet: bony fishes, cephalopods, crustaceans.

A common thresher shark *(Alopias vulpinus)* swims at the surface. *Photo by Ann Coleman / Monterey Bay Aquarium.*

Habitat: pelagic, on continental shelves, at depths ranging from 0 to at least 366 m (1,200 ft). Juveniles occur in shallower waters than adults.

Distribution in the area: all Oregon, Washington and British Columbia waters.

Distribution in the rest of the world: Atlantic, Pacific and Indian Oceans.

Behavior: particularly active and fast (thanks to their heat-retaining systems), occur singly or in groups, migratory, timid, can leap out of the water, can segregate by sex, use the long caudal fin upper lobe to slash the water in order to herd and disorient schooling fish on which they prey.

Threat to humans: not dangerous.

Notes: The common thresher shark is seasonally migratory with adult males tending to travel farther northward than females and reaching the coast of British Columbia by late summer. Subadult thresher sharks move as far north as the Columbia River area. The common thresher shark became the object of an important targeted pelagic gillnet fishery off Washington and Oregon in the late 1970s, peaking in the early 1980s and declining due to overfishing later that decade. The targeted fishery was ended by 1990 but the species was still caught as bycatch of the swordfish gillnet fishery. A management plan, created by researchers from California, Oregon and Washington, was developed for the common thresher shark. The resulting reduction in fishing pressure may have contributed to a rebuilding of the stock.

Basking shark

Cetorhinus maximus Gunnerus, 1765

Classification: order Lamniformes, family Cetorhinidae, genus *Cetorhinus*.

Morphology: Mouth very wide. 5 pairs of very long gill slits, extending up to the ventral and dorsal surfaces of the head, all located anteriorly to the pectoral fin origin; gillrakers present on its internal gill slits. Pectoral fins wide but moderately long. First dorsal fin very large, its origin posterior to pectoral fin free rear tip. Second dorsal small. Anal fin about as large as the second dorsal. Caudal fin lunate, with the upper lobe long and the lower lobe relatively short. Wide caudal keels. Snout long and conical, in juveniles has

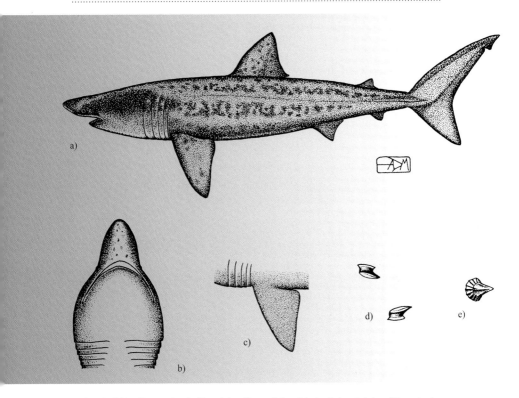

Basking shark (*Cetorhinus maximus*): a) lateral view, b) ventral view of the head, c) ventral view of the pectoral fin, d) upper and lower teeth, e) placoid scale. *Drawings by Alessandro De Maddalena.*

its tip narrow and curved. Eyes small. Spiracles very small.

Coloration: dorsal surfaces brown-gray with irregular dark patches; ventral surfaces similar to the dorsal surfaces or sometimes lighter. The pectoral fin ventral surface is dark like the dorsal surface. Juveniles have the ventral surfaces partially white, with the boundary separating dark from white coloration sharp and indented. Rare cases of albino specimens exist.

Teeth shape: upper teeth with one cusp, curved, very small and numerous; lower teeth similar.

Dental formula: about 100 – about 100 / about 100 – about 100.

Maximum size: 980 cm (386 in) and probably up to 1,200 cm (472 in).

Size at birth: about 150 cm (59 in).

Size at maturity: male: 460–601 cm (181–237 in); female: 800 cm (315 in).

Embryonic development: aplacental viviparous (maybe embryos nourished by oophagy).

A basking shark (*Cetorhinus maximus*). Photo by Chris Gotschalk.

Gestation: unknown, probably 1–3 years.

Litter size: 1–6 young.

Maximum age: possibly at least 16 years.

Diet: planktonic organisms including crustaceans, bony fish eggs, siphonophores and jellyfishes.

Habitat: pelagic, on continental and insular shelves at depths ranging from 0 to at least 200 m (656 ft). Scarcity of pregnant females and newborns suggests that they are spatially and bathymetrically separated from the rest of their populations.

Distribution in the area: all Oregon, Washington and British Columbia waters; in Alaska its range extends northward to Gulf of Alaska.

Distribution in the rest of the world: Atlantic, Pacific and Indian Oceans.

Behavior: active and slow, diurnal, occur singly or in small to enormous groups (over 500 specimens), migratory, can leap out of the water, can approach divers closely (without showing any aggressive behavior), possibly can segregate by sex (possibly even bathymetrically), usually swim at the surface with their mouths wide open to filter water and capture the planktonic organisms on which they feed thanks to their gillrakers, periodically shed their gillrakers in winter when plankton levels are low (replacement takes 4–5 months), during mating the male places its pectoral fin over the female's first dorsal fin and swims very close to her while inserting the clasper.

Threat to humans: not dangerous.

Notes: Basking sharks are scarce in the Pacific Northwest. These large sharks appear in Washington and British Columbia waters in spring and summer. During World War II, this species became a nuisance to British Columbia's commercial nets. In 1953 BC newspapers reported stories of Barkley Sound basking sharks destroying the gillnets of many fishermen. In 1955 the BC Department of Fisheries installed a cutting blade on the bow of the regional fisheries patrol vessel, the *Comox Post*. When the vessel approached a school of basking sharks the knife would be lowered from a hinge by a cable so that the cutting edge was just below the surface of the water and sharks cruising on the surface would be sliced in half. The blade was used over a period of 14 years in the Barkley Sound region, and killed over 400 basking sharks. Other fisheries patrol vessels were under directives from the federal Department of Fisheries to ram and kill the sharks. The press endorsed the eradication of this species, and the general public was urged to help with the elimination effort by means of recreational harpooning, shooting and ramming. Several hundred basking sharks were also killed by entanglement in gillnets, and it is not possible to estimate the number of these sharks killed for sport in the 1940s through to the mid-1960s. Today, sightings of basking sharks off British Columbia are extremely rare.

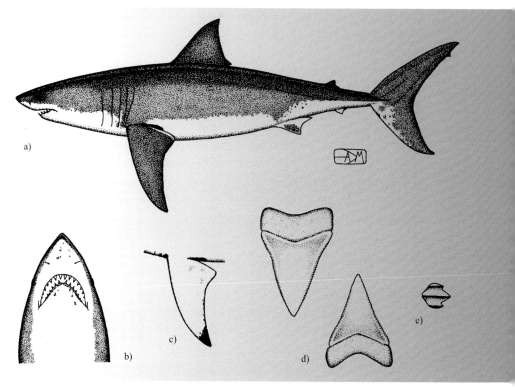

Great white shark (*Carcharodon carcharias*): a) lateral view, b) ventral view of the head, c) ventral view of the pectoral fin, d) upper and lower teeth, e) placoid scale. *Drawings by Alessandro De Maddalena.*

Great white shark
Carcharodon carcharias Linnaeus, 1758

Classification: order Lamniformes, family Lamnidae, genus *Carcharodon*.

Morphology: body massive. Snout large and conical. Mouth wide. Eyes moderately large. Caudal fin lunate, with the upper lobe long and the lower lobe slightly shorter. First dorsal fin large, its origin over the pectoral fin inner margin. Second dorsal fin very small. Anal fin about as large as the second dorsal. Pectoral fins wide and long. Wide caudal keels. Spiracles very small or absent. 5 pairs of long gill slits, all located anteriorly to the pectoral fin origin.

Coloration: dorsal surfaces gray-brown, usually with the flanks lighter than the upper surfaces; ventral surfaces white. Boundary separating dorsal from ventral coloration sharp and indented. The pectoral fin ventral surface shows a black patch at the apex and a narrow black band at the posterior margin with some small black spots. At the pectoral fin axil there is a black or gray patch. Eyes dark. Rare cases of albino specimens exist.

Teeth shape: upper teeth with one cusp, large, wide, triangular, with strongly serrated edges; lower teeth similar but narrower. Teeth of the lower jaw protruding from the mouth and in view even when the mouth is closed. Newborn specimens have 2 very small cusplets both in upper and lower teeth, and the lower teeth without serrations.

Dental formula: 12 to 14 – 12 to 14 / 10 to 13 – 10 to 13.

Maximum size: at least 668 cm (263 in) and probably over 800 cm (315 in).

Size at birth: 120–151 cm (47–59 in).

Size at maturity: male: about 380 cm (150 in); female: about 450–500 cm (177–197 in).

A great white shark (*Carcharodon carcharias*). Photo by Vittorio Gabriotti.

Embryonic development: aplacental viviparous (embryos nourished by oophagy).

Gestation: unknown.

Litter size: 2–14 and probably up to 17 young.

Maximum age: at least 53 years.

Diet: bony fishes, elasmobranchs, marine mammals, molluscs, crustaceans, sea turtles, birds, carcasses.

Habitat: Pelagic, mainly on continental and insular shelves, at depths ranging from 0 to at least 1,280 m (4,200 ft).

Distribution in the area: all Oregon, Washington and British Columbia waters; in Alaska its range extends northward to Bering Sea.

Distribution in the rest of the world: Atlantic, Pacific and Indian Oceans.

Behavior: particularly active and fast (thanks to their heat-retaining systems), equally diurnal and nocturnal, occur singly and in pairs or in small to large groups around a food source, can leap out of the water, migratory, can approach divers closely (often without showing any aggressive behavior), possibly segregate by size and sex (possibly even bathymetrically), occasionally ingest inedible items, show a social hierarchy when feeding, perform a threat display with jaws slightly open and pectoral fins depressed, raise the head out of the water to observe an object of interest, perform both horizontal- or vertical-oriented attacks on a prey by swimming rapidly from deep waters, use predatory tactics that enable them to eat their prey with minimal risk of injury and minimal energy expenditure (initial attack by surprise followed by waiting period while the prey dies from blood loss, then return within some minutes to eat the animal), during mating male and female stay belly to belly while inserting the clasper.

Threat to humans: highly dangerous.

Notes: The great white shark occurs occasionally in Pacific Northwest waters. Recent studies indicate that they are more abundant in the area than previous records suggest. Great white sharks recorded from British Columbia and Alaska waters are generally large, between 3.8 and 5.4 m (12–18 ft) in length. Diet includes salmon, Pacific halibut, hakes, rockfish, Steller sea lion, harbor seal and crabs. Strandings of these sharks are occasionally reported.

Shortfin mako

Isurus oxyrinchus Rafinesque, 1809

Classification: order Lamniformes, family Lamnidae, genus *Isurus*.

Morphology: body strongly spindle-shaped (quite slender in young but more massive in adults). Snout conical, narrow, long and strongly pointed. Caudal fin lunate, with the upper lobe long and the lower lobe slightly shorter. First dorsal fin tall, its origin posterior to pectoral fin free rear tip. Second dorsal very small. Anal fin about as large as the second dorsal. Pectoral fins relatively short (about 70 percent of the head length). Wide caudal keels. Mouth long but narrow in ventral view. Eyes relatively large. Spiracles very small. 5 pairs of long gill slits, all located anteriorly to the pectoral fin origin.

Coloration: dorsal surfaces brilliant blue to black with pronounced metallic reflections on the sides; ventral surfaces white. Boundary

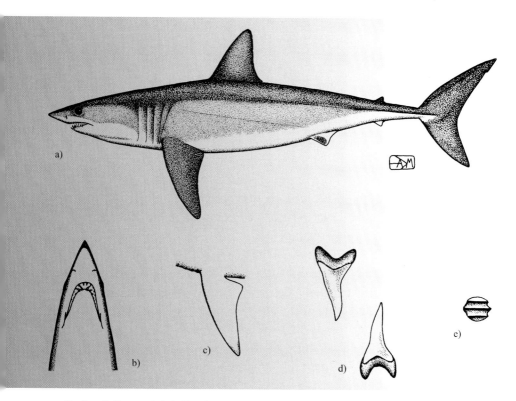

Shortfin mako (*Isurus oxyrinchus*): a) lateral view, b) ventral view of the head, c) ventral view of the pectoral fin, d) upper and lower teeth, e) placoid scale. *Drawings by Alessandro De Maddalena.*

107

A shortfin mako (*Isurus oxyrinchus*). *Photo by Walter Heim.*

separating dorsal from ventral coloration sharp. The pectoral fin ventral surface is white, sometimes with a small light grayish area at the apex and posterior margin. Eyes black.

Teeth shape: upper teeth with one cusp, large, narrow, long and curved, with cutting edges; lower teeth similar. Teeth of the lower jaw protruding from the mouth and in view even when the mouth is closed.

Dental formula: 12 to 14 – 12 to 14 / 11 to 15 – 11 to 15.

Maximum size: 445 cm (175 in).

Size at birth: 60–70 cm (24–28 in).

Size at maturity: male: about 195 cm (77 in); female: about 273–298 cm (107–117 in).

Embryonic development: aplacental viviparous (embryos nourished by oophagy).

Gestation: 15–18 months.

Litter size: 4–25 young.

Maximum age: at least 25 years.

Diet: bony fishes, elasmobranchs, marine turtles, squids, crustaceans, marine mammals, birds, salps, porifera, carcasses.

Habitat: pelagic, on continental and insular shelves, upper slopes and oceanic basins, at depths ranging from 0 to at least 417 m (1,368 ft). Juveniles occur in shallower waters than adults.

Distribution in the area: all Oregon, Washington and British Columbia waters; in Alaska its range extends northward to Aleutian Islands.

Distribution in the rest of the world: Atlantic, Pacific and Indian Oceans.

Behavior: nervous, particularly active and fast (thanks to their heat-retaining systems), occur singly or in large groups, migratory, can leap out of the water, timid, rarely approach divers closely (sometimes without showing any aggressive behavior), can segregate by size, occasionally ingest inedible items.

Threat to humans: dangerous.

Notes: Shortfin makos are relatively common in the Pacific Northwest. They move northward seasonally following warm water masses. In Oregon and Washington waters these sharks are caught in drift gillnet fisheries for swordfish and sharks. Shortfin makos are not thought to be sufficiently abundant to support a directed fishery, but they do occur as bycatch in the drift gillnet fishery in sufficient numbers to provide a marketable resource for that fishery. The market price for shortfin makos is high enough to ensure that they are landed. These sharks are also taken by recreational anglers.

Salmon shark

Lamna ditropis Hubbs & Follett, 1947

Classification: order Lamniformes, family Lamnidae, genus *Lamna.*

Morphology: body spindle-shaped, stout and massive. Snout conical and pointed. Caudal fin lunate, with the upper lobe long and the lower slightly shorter. First dorsal fin large to very large, its origin over the pectoral fin inner margin. Second dorsal fin very small. Anal fin about as large as the second dorsal. Pectoral fins relatively short. Two pairs of caudal keels: one wide on the caudal peduncle and another small on the sides of the caudal fin, immediately below the caudal peduncle. Mouth relatively small. Eyes relatively large. Spiracles very small or absent. 5 pairs of long gill slits, all located anteriorly to the pectoral fin origin.

Coloration: dorsal surfaces dark gray to bluish black; ventral surfaces

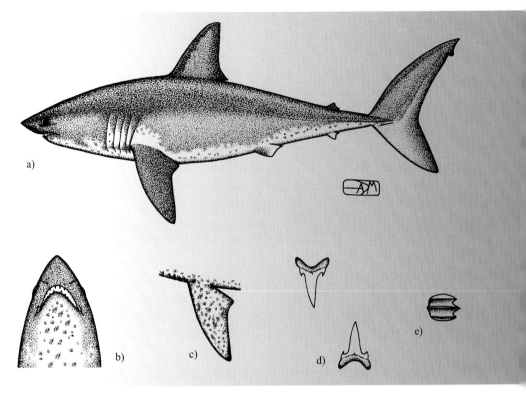

Salmon shark (*Lamna ditropis*): a) lateral view, b) ventral view of the head, c) ventral view of the pectoral fin, d) upper and lower teeth, e) placoid scale. *Drawings by Alessandro De Maddalena.*

white with numerous small gray spots. The first dorsal fin free rear tip has a conspicuous white patch. Ventral surface of pectoral fins with dark apex, margins and dark spots. Boundary separating dorsal from ventral coloration sharp and indented. Eyes black.

Teeth shape: upper teeth relatively small, with one cusp and two small cusplets with cutting edges; lower teeth similar. Teeth of the lower jaw protruding from the mouth and in view even when the mouth is closed. Teeth of juveniles may lack cusplets.

Dental formula: 14 to 16 – 14 to 16 / 13 to 15 – 13 to 15.

Maximum size: 305 cm (120 in).

Size at birth: 65–80 cm (25–31 in).

Size at maturity: male: 180–240 cm (71–94 in); female: 194–250 (76–98 in).

Embryonic development: aplacental viviparous (embryos nourished by oophagy).

Gestation: 12 months.

Litter size: 2–5 young.

Maximum age: 30 years.

Diet: bony fishes, cartilaginous fishes, squids.

Habitat: pelagic, on continental shelves and oceanic basins, at depths ranging from 0 to at least 668 m (2,192 ft).

Distribution in the area: all Oregon, Washington and British Columbia waters; in Alaska its range extends northward to Bering Sea.

Distribution in the rest of the world: Pacific Ocean.

Behavior: particularly active and fast (thanks to their heat-retaining systems), occur singly or in large groups (up to 40 specimens), hunt cooperatively in packs to capture schooling prey, migratory, can leap out of the water, timid, can segregate by sex and size.

Threat to humans: potentially dangerous.

Notes: Salmon sharks are common in the Pacific Northwest. They segregate in distribution by size and sex and conduct seasonal migrations, with larger salmon sharks going to more northern waters. Many fishermen view the salmon shark as a pest because of its frequent damage to fishing gear, particularly in salmon fisheries. Pacific salmon are the principal prey found in salmon shark stomachs collected during summer months in Prince William Sound, Alaska, but they also feed on sablefish, gadids, Pacific herring,

Salmon shark
(Lamna ditropis).
Photo by Scot Anderson.

111

rockfish and squid. Salmon sharks congregate at the adult migration routes and in the spawning grounds of Pacific salmon in Alaska during summer and expand their range southward in the winter and spring. Salmon sharks have been investigated as potential target species in the Gulf of Alaska, but due to the lack of biological knowledge on this species and increased sport fishing for it, the Alaska Board of Fisheries closed all commercial shark fishing in Alaskan waters and imposed heavy regulations on the sport fishery for salmon sharks in 1997. Recent research indicated that the north Pacific salmon shark population has recovered since the late 1990s. Thus, there is a possibility that the current increase in their abundance in the whole region of the north Pacific has increased mortality of salmon. Researchers suggest the continuation of monitoring studies to further understand how changes made to management of the salmon shark fishery can affect the ecosystem.

Brown catshark

Apristurus brunneus Gilbert, 1892

Classification: order Carcharhiniformes, family Scyliorhinidae, genus *Apristurus*.
Morphology: body elongated and slender. Dorsal fins small and of

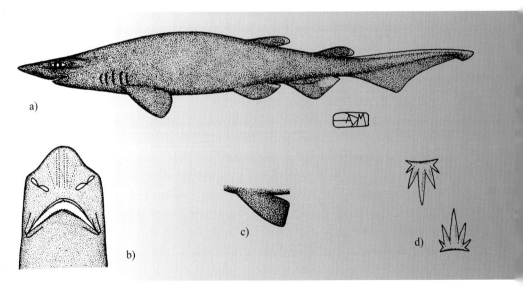

Brown catshark (*Apristurus brunneus*): a) lateral view, b) ventral view of the head, c) ventral view of the pectoral fin, d) upper and lower teeth. *Drawings by Alessandro De Maddalena.*

similar size, located backwards, the origin of the first dorsal fin over the pelvic fins. Caudal fin with short lower lobe and moderately long upper lobe, elongated on the axis of the body and with relatively wide terminal lobe. Anal fin very long, reaching the base of the caudal fin. Pectoral fins short. Snout long and dorso-ventrally flattened. Eyes large. Nostrils very wide. Internarial space about equal to the nostril width. Upper labial folds longer than lower. Spiracles relatively small. 5 pairs of short gill slits, the 4th and 5th over the pectoral fin base.

Brown catshark *(Apristurus brunneus)*. *Photo by Phil Edgell.*

Coloration: dorsal surfaces dark brown; ventral surfaces similar. Fin posterior margins darker.

Teeth shape: upper teeth very small, with one cusp and 2–4 cusplets, with smooth edges; lower teeth similar.

Dental formula: 29 to 37 – 29 to 37 / 24 to 34 – 24 to 34.

Maximum size: 69 cm (27 in).

Size at birth: 7–9 cm (2.75–3.5 in) at hatching.

Size at maturity: male: 45–50 cm (18–19.5 in); female: 42–48 cm (16.5–19 in).

Embryonic development: oviparous. Their eggs are 5 cm (2 in) long, 2.5 cm (1 in) wide, and are furnished with long tendrils and a translucent brown coloration.

Gestation: the egg cases' hatching time is 27 months.

Litter size: 2 young.

Maximum age: unknown.

Diet: crustaceans, cephalopods, bony fishes.

Habitat: benthic, mainly in deep waters, on outer continental shelves and upper slopes, at depths ranging from 33 to at least 1,298 m (108–4,258 ft).

Distribution in the area: all Oregon, Washington and British Columbia waters; in Alaska its range extends northward to Alexander Archipelago.

Distribution in the rest of the world: eastern Pacific Ocean.

Behavior: unknown.

Threat to humans: not dangerous.

Notes: Brown catsharks are common in Oregon, Washington and British Columbia waters. In BC waters this deep-sea catshark is more common in the Strait of Georgia at depths of 137 to 369 m (449–1,210 ft), but west of Barkley Sound off Vancouver Island it has been collected at a maximum depth of 564 m (1,850 ft). This shark has been frequently collected in bottom trawls in Astoria Canyon, at a maximum depth of 549 m (1,801 ft). Brown catsharks recorded from British Columbia waters are generally between 26 and 58 cm (10–23 in) in length. In the Pacific Northwest, they feed on crustaceans, squids and fish. Occasionally their egg cases are found in the material brought up by trawls in the Pacific Northwest, including Puget Sound, Washington. In British Columbia the period of ovulation extends from February to August.

Longnose catshark

Apristurus kampae Taylor, 1972

Classification: order Carcharhiniformes, family Scyliorhinidae, genus *Apristurus*.

Morphology: body elongated and slender. Dorsal fins small and of similar size, located backwards, the origin of the first dorsal fin over the pelvic fins. Caudal fin with short lower lobe and moderately long upper lobe, elongated on the axis of the body and with relatively wide terminal lobe. Anal fin very long, but doesn't reach the base of the caudal fin. Pectoral fins short. Snout long and dorso-ventrally flattened. Eyes large. Nostrils relatively wide. Internarial space larger than the nostril width. Lower labial folds longer than upper. Spiracles relatively small. 5 pairs of short gill slits, the 4th and 5th over the pectoral fin base.

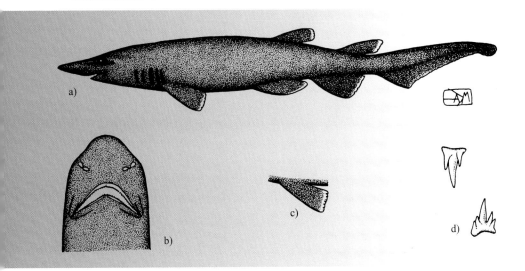

Longnose catshark (*Apristurus kampae*): a) lateral view, b) ventral view of the head, c) ventral view of the pectoral fin, d) upper and lower teeth. *Drawings by Alessandro De Maddalena.*

Coloration: dorsal surfaces dark brown to black; ventral surfaces similar. Fins with white posterior margins. The inside of the mouth is bluish black.

Teeth shape: upper teeth very small, with one cusp and 2–6 cusplets, with smooth edges; lower teeth similar.

Dental formula: 24 to 29 – 24 to 29 / 18 to 26 – 18 to 26.

Maximum size: 57 cm (22 in).

Size at birth: about 14 cm (5.5 in) at hatching.

Size at maturity: male: 50 cm (19.5 in); female: 48–52 cm (19–20 in).

Embryonic development: oviparous. Their eggs are 7 cm (2.75 in) long, and are furnished with long tendrils.

Gestation: unknown.

Litter size: 2 young.

Maximum age: unknown.

Diet: crustaceans, cephalopods, bony fishes.

Habitat: benthic, mainly in deep waters, on outer continental shelves and slopes, at depths ranging from 180 to at least 1,888 m (590–6,194 ft).

Distribution in the area: Oregon; its range extends northward to Capo Blanco.

Distribution in the rest of the world: eastern Pacific Ocean.

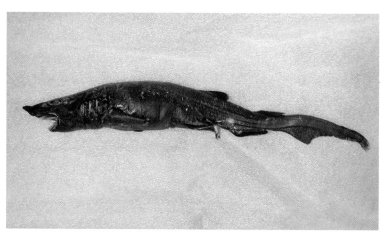

Longnose catshark *(Apristurus kampae)* preserved in the University of Washington Fish Collection (catalog number UW 045805). *Photo by Katherine Pearson Maslenikov, courtesy of the University of Washington Fish Collection.*

Behavior: unknown.

Threat to humans: not dangerous.

Notes: In Oregon waters, this little-known deepwater shark is less common than the brown catshark and usually occurs at greater depths. Egg cases of longnose catshark have been found in the material brought up by trawls off Oregon. Because of the depth at which this species is typically found, knowledge is extremely limited concerning the life history of these catsharks.

Filetail catshark

Parmaturus xaniurus Gilbert, 1892

Classification: order Carcharhiniformes, family Scyliorhinidae, genus *Parmaturus*.

Morphology: body elongated and slender. Dorsal fins small and of

Filetail catshark *(Parmaturus xaniurus)* swimming just above the bottom at a depth of about 1,000 m (3,280 ft). *Photo © 2005 MBARI.*

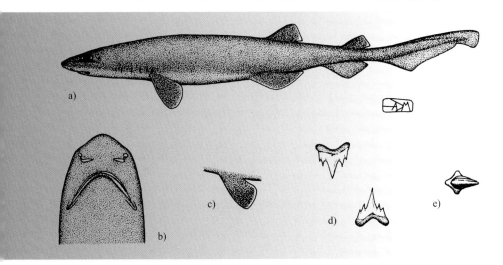

Filetail catshark (*Parmaturus xaniurus*): a) lateral view, b) ventral view of the head, c) ventral view of the pectoral fin, d) upper and lower teeth, e) placoid scale. *Drawings by Alessandro De Maddalena.*

similar size, located backwards, the origin of the first dorsal fin over the pelvic fins. Caudal fin with short lower lobe and moderately long upper lobe, elongated on the axis of the body and with relatively wide terminal lobe; anterior margin of upper caudal lobe with a prominent row of enlarged dermal denticles. Anal fin relatively long. Pectoral fins short. Snout short and rounded. Eyes large. Nostrils relatively wide. Spiracles relatively small. 5 pairs of short gill slits, the 4th and 5th over the pectoral fin base.

Coloration: dorsal surfaces brownish black; ventral surfaces slightly lighter; a light band above the pelvic fins extends toward the caudal region. Fins have white posterior margins. The lining of the mouth cavity is white.

Teeth shape: upper teeth very small, with one cusp and 2–6 cusplets, with smooth edges; lower teeth similar.

Dental formula: 33 to 45 – 33 to 45 / 42 – 42.

Maximum size: 61 cm (24 in).

Size at birth: 7–9 cm (2.75–3.5 in) at hatching.

Size at maturity: male: 34–43 cm (13–17 in); female: 42–48 cm (16.5–19 in).

Embryonic development: oviparous. Their eggs are 7–11 cm (2.75–4 in) long, 3 cm (1.25 in) wide, and are furnished with long tendrils, a T-shaped flange running along its lateral edges, and a tan coloration.

Gestation: about 12 months.

Litter size: 2 young.

Maximum age: unknown.

Diet: bony fishes, crustaceans.

Habitat: benthic, mainly in deep waters, on outer continental shelves and upper slopes, at depths ranging from 91 to at least 1,251 m (300–4,100 ft).

Distribution in the area: Oregon; its range extends northward to Cape Foulweather.

Distribution in the rest of the world: eastern Pacific Ocean.

Behavior: is able to live in low-oxygen areas inhabited by a few other vertebrates.

Threat to humans: not dangerous.

Notes: Egg cases of filetail catshark have been found in the material brought up by trawls off Oregon. The filetail catshark is not targeted by commercial fisheries, but is known to be incidental catch in longline and bottom trawl fisheries, although it is not used for human consumption. Because of the depth at which this species is typically found, knowledge is extremely limited concerning the life history of these catsharks.

Tope shark or soupfin shark
Galeorhinus galeus Linnaeus, 1758

Classification: order Carcharhiniformes, family Triakidae, genus *Galeorhinus*.

Morphology: first dorsal fin large, its origin over the pectoral fin inner margin or posterior to pectoral fin free rear tip. Second dorsal fin small. Anal fin about as large as the second dorsal. Pectoral fins relatively short. Caudal fin with relatively long lower lobe and long upper lobe with enormous terminal lobe. Underside of head strongly flattened. Snout long. Upper labial folds short. Nostrils relatively small. Eyes large and located dorsally on the head. Spiracles small. 5 pairs of short gill slits, the 5th located over the pectoral fin base.

Coloration: dorsal surfaces brown-gray, sometimes with slightly darker spots; ventral surfaces white. The pectoral fin ventral surface is white in the basal part and partially gray-brown, with a darker band parallel to the posterior margin and a narrow whitish band adjacent

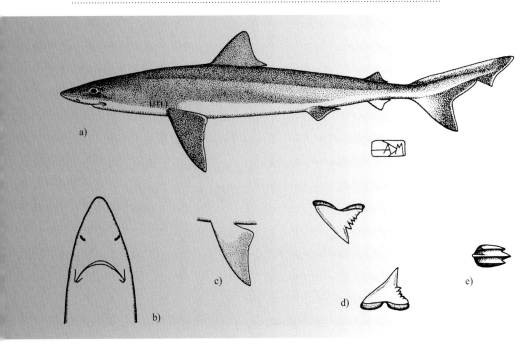

Tope shark (*Galeorhinus galeus*): a) lateral view, b) ventral view of the head, c) ventral view of the pectoral fin, d) upper and lower teeth, e) placoid scale. *Drawings by Alessandro De Maddalena.*

to the posterior margin. Rare cases of albino specimens exist.

Teeth shape: upper teeth with one cusp, with the medial edge cutting and the lateral edge partially serrated; lower teeth similar.

Dental formula: 17 to 20 – 17 to 20 / 15 to 23 – 15 to 23.

Maximum size: 195 cm (77 in).

Size at birth: 30–40 cm (12–16 in).

Size at maturity: male: 120 cm (47 in); female: 130–150 cm (51–59 in).

Embryonic development: aplacental viviparous.

Gestation: 10–12 months.

Litter size: 6–52 young.

Maximum age: 60 years.

Diet: bony fishes, cephalopods, crustaceans, anellids, echinoderms, jellyfishes, elasmobranchs, carcasses.

Habitat: on continental and insular shelves, at depths ranging from 0 to at least 598 m (1,962 ft). Pregnant females give birth close inshore, where juveniles often remain, while males stay in deeper waters.

Tope shark (*Galeorhinus galeus*). *Photo by Cindy Hanson, courtesy of Oregon Coast Aquarium.*

Distribution in the area: all Oregon, Washington and British Columbia waters.

Distribution in the rest of the world: Atlantic, Pacific and Indian Oceans.

Behavior: active, occur singly or in small groups, migratory, timid, can segregate by sex and size.

Threat to humans: not dangerous.

Notes: Tope sharks are common in the Pacific Northwest. Tagging studies on these sharks have demonstrated extensive movements. In Oregon and Washington waters these sharks are caught in drift gillnet fisheries for swordfish and sharks. In the 1930s and 1940s tope sharks were intensively fished for their vitamin A-rich liver until the vitamin was synthesized. Catch of this species has declined substantially since the early 1990s. This decline was a reflection of a decline in fishing effort, rising mesh size and legislative requirements for the fleet to operate progressively farther offshore. There are also demersal trawl fisheries in Oregon that take a bycatch of tope sharks, and they are also taken as part of the recreational fishery.

Brown smoothhound

Mustelus henlei Gill, 1863

Classification: order Carcharhiniformes, family Triakidae, genus *Mustelus*.

Morphology: first dorsal fin large, its origin over the pectoral fin free rear tip. The first dorsal fin has a thin, frayed rear edge. Second dorsal slightly smaller. Anal fin much smaller than second dorsal. Pectoral fins relatively short but wide. Caudal fin with short lower lobe and moderately long upper lobe with large terminal lobe. Body relatively slender. Underside of head strongly flattened. Snout long. Nostrils wide. Eyes large and located dorsally on the head. Spiracles medium-sized. 5 pairs of short gill slits, the 4th and 5th located over the pectoral fin base.

Coloration: dorsal surfaces iridescent bronzy-brown or gray, sometimes with minute dark spots; ventral surfaces white.

Teeth shape: upper teeth small, with one cusp and 0–1 cusplets; lower teeth similar.

Dental formula: 30 to 40 – 30 to 40 / 27 to 39 – 27 to 39.

Maximum size: 100 cm (39 in).

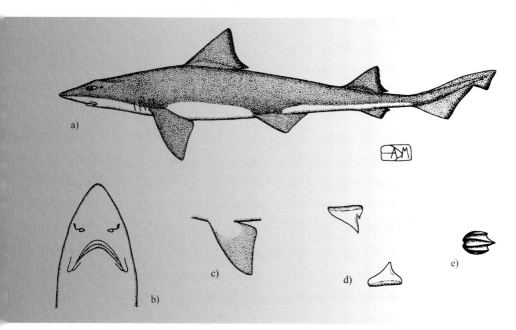

Brown smoothhound (*Mustelus henlei*): a) lateral view, b) ventral view of the head, c) ventral view of the pectoral fin, d) upper and lower teeth, e) placoid scale. *Drawings by Alessandro De Maddalena.*

Brown
smoothhound
(*Mustelus henlei*).
Photo by Bob Fenner.

Size at birth: 19–30 cm (7.5–12 in).

Size at maturity: male: 52–66 cm (20–26 in); female: 51–63 cm (20–25 in).

Embryonic development: placental viviparous.

Gestation: 10–11 months.

Litter size: 1–10 young.

Maximum age: at least 13 years.

Diet: crustaceans, squids, bony fishes, polichetes, tunicates.

Habitat: benthic, on continental shelves, at depths ranging from 0 to at least 200 m (656 ft).

Distribution in the area: Oregon; its range extends northward to Coos Bay.

Distribution in the rest of the world: eastern Atlantic Ocean.

Behavior: active, occur singly or in groups, can segregate by sex and size.

Threat to humans: not dangerous.

Notes: Brown smoothhounds are relatively common in Oregon waters, predominantly inshore and in shallow bays and estuaries. These sharks are occasionally taken incidentally with trawl or longline gear, and also by recreational anglers.

Leopard shark

Triakis semifasciata Girard, 1854

Classification: order Carcharhiniformes, family Triakidae, genus *Triakis*.

Morphology: first dorsal fin large, its origin over the pectoral fin free rear tip. Second dorsal slightly smaller. Anal fin much smaller than second dorsal. Pectoral fins relatively short but wide. Caudal fin with short lower lobe and relatively long upper lobe with large terminal lobe. Body relatively slender. Underside of the head strongly flattened. Snout moderately long. Nostrils very wide. Eyes large and located dorsally on the head. Spiracles medium-sized. 5 pairs of short gill slits, the 4th and 5th located over the pectoral fin base.

Coloration: dorsal surfaces grayish brown to bronze gray with large black to grayish brown saddle marks and spots that are light centered in adults; ventral surfaces white. The pectoral fin ventral surface is grayish brown like the dorsal surfaces. Rare cases of albino specimens exist.

Teeth shape: upper teeth very small, with one cusp and 1–2 cusplets; lower teeth similar.

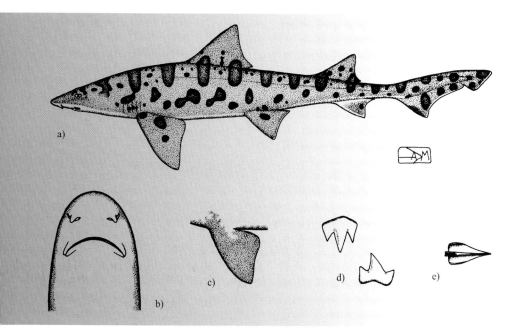

Leopard shark (*Triakis semifasciata*): a) lateral view, b) ventral view of the head, c) ventral view of the pectoral fin, d) upper and lower teeth, e) placoid scale. *Drawings by Alessandro De Maddalena.*

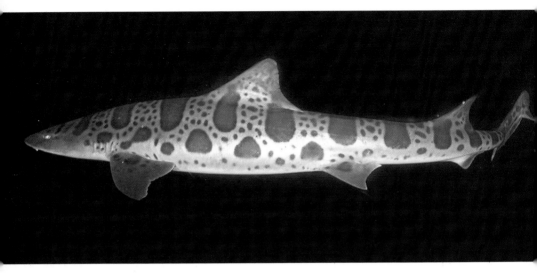

Leopard shark (*Triakis semifasciata*). Photo by Cindy Hanson, courtesy of Oregon Coast Aquarium.

Dental formula: 20 to 27 – 20 to 27 / 17 to 22 – 17 to 22.

Maximum size: 210 cm (83 in).

Size at birth: 20 cm (8 in).

Size at maturity: male: 70–119 cm (28–47 in); female: 110–129 cm (43–51 in).

Embryonic development: aplacental viviparous.

Gestation: 10–12 months.

Litter size: 4–36 young.

Maximum age: at least 24 years.

Diet: crustaceans, molluscs, bony fishes, elasmobranchs, polichetes, algae.

Habitat: benthic, on continental shelves, at depths ranging from 0 to at least 91 m (298 ft).

Distribution in the area: Oregon.

Distribution in the rest of the world: eastern Pacific Ocean.

Behavior: active, occur singly or in large groups, can segregate by sex and size.

Threat to humans: not dangerous.

Notes: Leopard sharks are relatively common in Oregon waters, and form large schools that seem to be nomadic. Sometimes seen together with brown smoothhounds or piked dogfish. Feed primarily on bottom-living invertebrates. These sharks are occasionally taken incidentally with trawl or longline gear. Management of this species in recent years is thought to have protected their population in Oregon waters.

Blue shark

Prionace glauca Linnaeus, 1758

Classification: order Carcharhiniformes, family Carcharhinidae, genus *Prionace*.

Morphology: first dorsal fin relatively large, its origin well posterior to the pectoral fin free rear tip. Second dorsal small. Anal fin about as large as the second dorsal. Pectoral fins very long and narrow. Caudal fin with moderately long lower lobe and much longer upper lobe with large terminal lobe. Small caudal keels. Body slender. No interdorsal ridge. Snout very long and narrow. Mouth wide and parabolic in ventral view. Labial folds short. Eyes large. Nostrils small. No spiracles. 5 pairs of short gill slits, the 4th and 5th located over the pectoral fin base.

Coloration: dorsal surfaces bright blue; ventral surfaces white. The fin apex and posterior margins have a narrow and inconspicuous black band. The pectoral fin ventral surface is white with a small

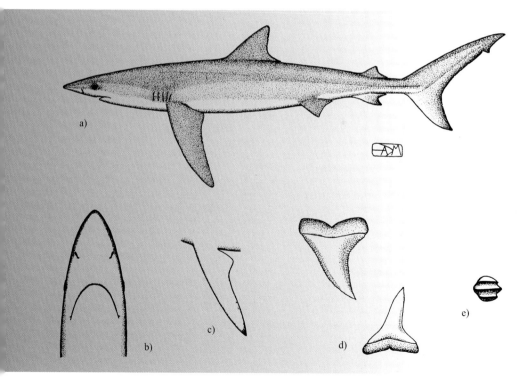

Blue shark (*Prionace glauca*): a) lateral view, b) ventral view of the head, c) ventral view of the pectoral fin, d) upper and lower teeth, e) placoid scale. *Drawings by Alessandro De Maddalena.*

The blue shark *(Prionace glauca)* is common in Pacific Northwest waters, up to Vancouver Island, and can be found further north during the summer months. *Photo © www.davidfleetham.com.*

black patch at the apex and a narrow black band on the posterior margin.

Teeth shape: upper teeth with one cusp, large, long, relatively narrow, curved, oblique, with strongly serrated edges; lower teeth with one cusp, narrower, oblique, with edges finely serrated in the upper part and smooth at the base.

Dental formula: 13 to 16 – 1 to 2 – 13 to 16 / 13 to 16 – 1 to 4 – 13 to 16.

Maximum size: 383 cm (151 in).

Size at birth: 35–52 cm (14–20 in).

Size at maturity: male: 175–281 cm (69–110.5 in); female: 145–221 cm (57–87 in).

Embryonic development: placental viviparous.

Gestation: 9–12 months.

Litter size: 3–135 young.

Maximum age: at least 20 years.

Diet: molluscs, bony fishes and their eggs, sharks, crustaceans, cetaceans, nematods, birds, carcasses.

Habitat: pelagic, on continental and insular shelves and oceanic basins, at depths ranging from 0 to at least 610 m (2,000 ft). They live offshore during the day but can move close inshore at night. Pregnant females give birth in shallower waters.

Distribution in the area: all Oregon, Washington and British Columbia waters; in Alaska its range extends northward to Gulf of Alaska.

Distribution in the rest of the world: Atlantic, Pacific and Indian Oceans.

Behavior: active and fast, primarily nocturnal, occur singly or in large to enormous groups around a source of food, migratory, can approach divers closely (usually without showing any aggressive behavior), can segregate by sex and size, feed on schooling fishes and squids by simply taking bites from the tightly massed prey and swimming through the school with mouths wide open and ingesting prey that inadvertently run into their jaws, females can preserve sperm for long periods.

Threat to humans: dangerous.

Notes: The blue shark is common in the Pacific Northwest, where it is present in greatest abundance up to Vancouver Island, British Columbia. It feeds on anchovy, mackerel, salmon, pomfret, saury,

lanternfish, daggertooth, hake, dogfish, squid and crustaceans. These sharks show strong fluctuations in seasonal abundance. Northward movements extend into the Gulf of Alaska as waters warm during the summer months, and southward movements occur during the winter months. There is considerable sexual segregation in populations, with females more abundant than males at higher latitudes. Mature females are thought to start their northward journey in early spring as warm water moves northward, while juveniles of both sexes follow closely; large males start later and tend to stay farther offshore. Blue sharks tagged off southern California have been recaptured northward off Oregon. Nursery habitat may extend northward to the waters off the Columbia River mouth. These sharks are frequently taken in the Oregon drift gillnet fishery for swordfish. Catch of this species has declined substantially since the early 1980s. Blue sharks are not landed in Washington and Oregon due to the lack of a market. These sharks are not marketed from the drift gillnet fishery as rapid spoilage occurs after death; usually they are discarded at sea.

Blue shark (*Prionace glauca*). Photo by Walter Heim.

About the Authors

Alessandro De Maddalena

Alessandro De Maddalena (Milan, 1970) is one of Europe's foremost shark experts. He is the curator of the Italian Great White Shark Data Bank, the President of the Italian Ichthyological Society and a founding member of the Mediterranean Shark Research Group. His research subjects include great white shark biology, sharks morphology, distribution and fishery. The results of his research have appeared in numerous scientific journals including *Annales Series historia naturalis, Museologia Scientifica, Annali del Museo Civico di Storia Naturale di Genova, Bollettino del Museo civico di Storia naturale di Venezia, Thalassia Salentina, Biljeske—Notes, Journal of the National Museum of Prague, South African Journal of Science, Marine Life*. He is the author of six other books on sharks: *Squali delle Acque Italiane* (Ireco, 2001), *Lo Squalo Bianco nei Mari d'Italia* (Ireco, 2002), *Sharks of the Adriatic Sea* (Knjiznica Annales Majora, 2004, co-authored with Lovrenc Lipej and Alen Soldo), *Mako Sharks* (Krieger Publishing, 2005, co-authored with Antonella Preti and Robert Smith), *Haie im Mittelmeer* (Kos-

Alessandro De Maddalena drawing the illustrations for the book. *Photo by Nicola Allegri.*

mos Verlag, 2005, co-authored with Harald Bänsch), *I grandi animali marini del Mediterraneo. Guida al loro riconoscimento in mare* (Rivista Marittima, 2005, co-authored with Antonio Celona). Alessandro De Maddalena is also one of the world's best wildlife illustrators; he has produced more than 800 drawings and paintings of sharks and cetaceans. His articles and illustrations have appeared in many wildlife magazines including *The World and I, Dive New Zealand, Dive Pacific, Annales, Biologie in unserer Zeit, Unterwasser, Apnéa, Plongeurs International, Océanorama, Enviromagazin, Mondo Sommerso, Il Pesce, EuroFishmarket, Aqva, Quark, Airone* and *Rivista Marittima.*

Contact:
Dr. Alessandro De Maddalena
Italian Great White Shark Data Bank
via L. Ariosto 4, I-20145 Milan, Italy
E-mail: a-demaddalena@tiscali.it
Website: http://www.geocities.com/demaddalena_a/demaddalena.html

Antonella Preti

Antonella Preti (Turin, 1971) graduated in biology, and specialized in marine ecology at the University of Turin, Italy, with a thesis on the genetics of polychaetes. In 1997, she moved to San Diego, California, to further her studies at the Scripps Institution of Oceanography. During her career she participated in various projects such as

Antonella Preti with a broadnose sevengill shark *(Notorynchus cepedianus)*. Photo by Roy Allen, courtesy of NMFS.

the census of the Mediterranean Cetaceans, the study of the behavior of the bottlenose dolphins in California, the construction of a model of growth and feeding behavior for the sheep crab, and the restoration of the Marine Ecological Reserve of Mission Bay, California. She participated in the study for the assessment of the biomass of Pacific sardines, finfish and squid on the west coast of the United States. In recent years she has been working on a study funded by the National Marine Fisheries Service in La Jolla, California, on the feeding behavior of the common thresher shark (*Alopias vulpinus*). She is currently working on a comparative feeding study of the shortfin mako, blue and common thresher sharks. She is involved in environmental education and is the founder of Cyber Sharks—an organization to conserve sharks worldwide. Cyber Sharks' goal is to raise awareness and change the negative image that sharks have been subjected to in the past. Antonella Preti is a member of the Mediterranean Shark Research Group.

Contact:
Dr. Antonella Preti
National Marine Fisheries Service, Southwest Fisheries Science Center
8604 La Jolla Shores Drive, La Jolla, CA 92037, USA
E-mail: sharksharkshark@hotmail.com
Web site: http://www.geocities.com/cybersharks2000

Tarik Polansky

Tarik Polansky (Oceanside, 1977) had his first introduction to sharks in the depths of a darkened movie theater. The sensationalism of the film *Jaws* inspired a great deal of reflection and contemplation for him at a very early age. He immediately identified with the great white and felt sympathy for a creature that was so hated in the film, and which later suffered a poor reputation due to the film's success. Since then, he has acquired a Bachelor of Arts in visual arts (media) from the University of California, San Diego, and has worked steadily in his field ever since. He is greatly concerned about the future of sharks and has made it his life's work to see that the truth is spoken and heard.

Contact:
Tarik Polansky
E-mail: tarik_p@yahoo.com
Web site: http://tarikpolansky.com

Tarik Polansky, on the coast of San Diego. *Photo by Antonella Preti.*

Bibliography

Acuña, E., and J.C. Villaroel. 2003. "Distribution, abundance and reproductive biology of the blue shark *Prionace glauca* in the Southeastern Pacific Ocean." *AES Abstracts Manaus, Brazil,* June 27–June 30: 36.

Adams, D.H., and R.H. McMichael Jr. 1999. "Mercury levels in four species of sharks from the Atlantic coast of Florida." *Fishery Bulletin,* 97: 372–379.

Alonso, M.K., E.A. Crespo, N.A. Garcia, S.N. Pedraza, P.A. Mariotti, and N.J. Mora. 2002. "Fishery and ontogenetic driven changes in the diet of the spiny dogfish, *Squalus acanthias,* in Patagonian waters, Argentina." *Environmental Biology of Fishes,* 63: 193–202.

Balart, E.F., J. González-García, and C. Villavicencio-Garayzar. 2000. "Notes on the biology of *Cephalurus cephalus* and *Parmaturus xaniurus* (Chondrichthyes: Scyliorhinidae) from the west coast of Baja California Sur, México." *Fishery Bulletin,* 98: 219–221.

Barrull, J., and I. Mate. 2000. "Biología de la cañabota *Hexanchus griseus* (Bonnaterre, 1788) en el Mar Mediterráneo." *Boletín de la Asociación Española de Elasmobranquios,* 3: 13–20.

_____. 2001. "Presence of the Great White Shark *Carcharodon carcharias* (Linnaeus, 1758) in the Catalonian Sea (NW Mediterranean): review and discussion of records, and notes about its ecology." *Annales, Series historia naturalis,* 11(1): 3–12.

_____. 2002. *Tiburones del Mediterráneo.* Llibreria El Set-ciències, Arenys de Mar, 292 pp.

Bass, A.J., J.D. D'Aubrey, and N. Kistnasamy. 1973–1976. "Sharks of the east coast of Southern Africa." 1–6, *Investigational Report of the Oceanographic Research Institute, Durban,* 33, 37, 38, 39, 43, 45.

Bauchot, M.L. 1987. "Requins." Pp. 767–843 in Fischer W., M. Schneider, and M.-L. Bauchot (eds.), *Fiches FAO d'identification des espèces pour les besoins de la peche. (Révision 1). Méditerranée et Mer Noire. Zone de peche 37. Vol. 2. Vertébrés.* Rome, CEE, FAO.

Bello, G. 1997. "Cephalopods from the stomach contents of demersal chondrichthyans caught in the Adriatic Sea." *Vie et milieu,* 47(3): 221–227.

Benz, G.W., J.D. Borucinska, L.F. Lowry, and H.E. Whiteley. 2002. "Ocular lesions associated with attachment of the copepod *Ommatokoita elongata* (Lernaeopodidae: Siphonostomatoida) to corneas of Pacific sleeper sharks *Somniosus pacificus* captured off Alaska in Prince William Sound." *The Journal of Parasitology,* 88(3): 474–481.

Benz, G.W., R. Hocking, A. Kowunna, S. Bullard, and J. George. 2004. "A second species of Arctic shark: Pacific sleeper shark *Somniosus pacificus* from Point Hope, Alaska." *Polar Biology,* 27(4): 250–252.

Benz, G.W., Z. Lucas, and L.F. Lowry. 1998. "New Host and Ocean Records for the Copepod *Ommatokoita elongata* (Siphonostomatoida: Lernaeopodidae), a Parasite of the Eyes of Sleeper Sharks." *The Journal of Parasitology,* 84(6): 1271–1274.

Bigelow, H.B., and W.C. Schroeder. 1948. "Sharks." In *Fishes of the Western North Atlantic. Part one: Lancelets, Ciclostomes, Sharks.* Memoir Sears Foundation for Marine Research, Yale University.

Bigelow, H.B., and W.C. Schroeder. 1957. "A study of the sharks of the suborder Squaloidea." *Bulletin of the Museum of Comparative Zoology, Harvard University*, 117(1): 1–150.

Bonfil, R. 1999. "The dogfish (*Squalus acanthias*) fishery of British Columbia, Canada and its management." Pp. 608–655 in Shotton, R. (ed.), *Case studies of the management of elasmobranch fisheries*. FAO Fisheries Technical Paper. No. 378, part 2. FAO, Rome, pp. 480–920.

Bosley, K.L., J.W. Lavelle, R.D. Brodeur, W.W. Wakefield, R.L. Emmett, E.T. Baker, and K.M. Rehmke. 2004. "Biological and Physical Processes in and around Astoria Submarine Canyon, Oregon, U.S.A." *Journal of Marine Systems*, 50: 21–37.

Brodeur, R.D., H.V. Lorz, and W.G. Pearcy. 1987. "Food habits and dietary variability of pelagic nekton off Oregon and Washington, 1979–1984." *NOAA Technical Report NMFS*, 57: 1–32.

Buencuerpo, V., S. Rios, and J. Morón. 1998. "Pelagic sharks associated with the swordfish, *Xiphias gladius*, fishery in the eastern North Atlantic Ocean and the Strait of Gibraltar." *Fishery Bulletin*, 96(4): 667–685.

Cadenat, J., and J. Blache. 1981. "Requins de Méditerranée et d'Atlantique (plus particulièrement de la Côte Occidentale d'Afrique)." *Faune Tropicale, ORSTOM, Paris*, 21: 1–330.

Capapé, C. 1974. "Observation sur la sexualité, la reproduction et la fécundité de 8 Sélaciens pleurotrêmes vivipares placentaires des côtes tunisiennes." *Archives de l'Institut Pasteur de Tunis*, 51(4): 329–344.

_____. 1975. "Observations sur le régime alimentaire de 29 Selaciens pleurotêrmes des côtes tunisiennes." *Archives de l'Institut Pasteur de Tunis*, 52(4): 395–414.

_____. 1989. "Les Sélaciens des côtes méditerranéennes: aspects generaux de leur écologie et exemples de peuplements." *Océanis*, 15 (3): 309–331.

Capapé, C., O. Guélorget, J. Barrull, I. Mate, F. Hemida, R. Seridji, J. Bensaci, and M. Nejmeddine Bradaï. 2003. "Records of the bluntnose six-gill shark, *Hexanchus griseus* (Bonnaterre, 1788) (Chondrichthyes: Hexanchidae) in the Mediterranean Sea: a historical survey." *Annales, Series historia naturalis*, 13(2): 157–166.

Capapé, C., F. Hemida, O. Guélorget, J. Barrull, I. Mate, J. Ben Souissi, and M. Nejmeddine Bradaï. 2003. "Reproductive biology of the bluntnose sixgill shark *Hexanchus griseus* (Bonnaterre, 1788) (Chondrichthyes: Hexanchidae) from the Mediterranean Sea: a review." *Acta Adriatica*, 45(1): 95–106.

Castro, J. 1983. *The Sharks of North American Waters*. Texas A&M University Press, College Station, 180 pp.

Celona, A., A. De Maddalena, and T. Romeo. 2005. "Bluntnose sixgill shark, *Hexanchus griseus* (Bonnaterre, 1788), in the eastern north Sicilian waters." *Bollettino del Museo Civico di Storia Naturale di Venezia*, 56: 137–151.

Celona, A., N. Donato, and A. De Maddalena. 2001. "In relation to the captures of a great white shark *Carcharodon carcharias* (Linnaeus, 1758) and a shortfin mako, *Isurus oxyrinchus* (Rafinesque, 1809) in the Messina Strait." *Annales, Series historia naturalis*, 11(1): 13–16.

Celona, A., L. Piscitelli, and A. De Maddalena. 2004. "Two large shortfin makos, *Isurus oxyrinchus*, Rafinesque, 1809, caught off Sicily, Western Ionian Sea." *Annales, Series historia naturalis*, 14(1): 35–42.

Clark, E., and E. Kristof. 1991. "How deep do sharks go? Reflections on deep sea sharks." Pp. 77–78 in Gruber S.H. (ed.), "Discovering sharks." *Underwater Naturalist, Bulletin American Littoral Society*, 19(4)–20(1).

Cliff, G., L.J.V. Compagno, M.J. Smale, R.P. Van Der Elst, and S.P. Wintner. 2000. "First records of white sharks, *Carcharodon carcharias*, from Mauritius, Zanzibar, Madagascar and Kenya." *South African Journal of Science*, 96: 365–367.

Cliff, G., S.F.J. Dudley, and B. Davis. 1989. "Sharks caught in the protective gill nets off Natal, South Africa. 2. The great white shark *Carcharodon carcharias* (Linnaeus)." *South African Journal of Marine Science*, 8: 131–144.

_____. 1989. "Sharks caught in the protective gill nets off Natal, South Africa. 3. The shortfin mako shark *Isurus oxyrinchus* (Linnaeus)." *South African Journal of Marine Science*, 9: 115–126.

Collier, R.S. 2003. *Shark Attacks of the Twentieth Century from the Pacific Coast of North America*. Scientia Publishing, LLC, Chatsworth, 296 pp.

Collier, R.S., M. Marks, and R.W. Warner. 1996. "White shark attacks on inanimate objects along the Pacific coast of North America." Pp. 217–221 in Klimley, A.P., and D.G. Ainley (eds.), *Great white sharks: The biology of* Carcharodon carcharias. Academic Press, San Diego, 518 pp.

Compagno, L.J.V. 1984. FAO Species Catalogue. Vol. 4. "Sharks of the World. An annotated and illustrated catalogue of sharks species known to date." Parts 1 and 2. *FAO Fisheries Synopsis*, 125: 1–655.

_____. 2001. *Sharks of the world. An annotated and illustrated catalogue of shark species known to date. Volume 2. Bullhead, mackerel and carpet sharks (Heterodontiformes, Lamniformes and Orectolobiformes)*. FAO Species Catalogue for Fishery Purposes. No. 1, Vol. 2. FAO, Rome, 269 pp.

Courtney, D.L., S. Gaichas, J. Boldt, K.J. Goldman, and C. Tribuzio. 2004. "Sharks in the Gulf of Alaska, Eastern Bering Sea, and Aleutian Islands." Appendix. Pp. 1009–1074 in *Stock assessment and fishery evaluation report for the Bering Sea and Aleutian Islands*. North Pacific Fishery Management Council, Anchorage.

Cousteau, J.P., and P. Cousteau. 1970. *The shark: splendid savage of the sea*. Cassell, London, 277 pp.

Delacy, A.C., and W.M. Chapman. 1935. "Notes on some elasmobranchs of Puget Sound, with descriptions of their egg cases." *Copeia*, 2: 63–67.

De La Serna, J.M., J. Valeiras, J.M. Ortiz, and D. Macias. 2002. "Large pelagic sharks as by-catch in the Mediterranean swordfish longline fishery: some biological aspects." *Northwest Atlantic Fisheries Organization, Scientific Council Meeting – September 2002*: 1–33.

De Maddalena, A. 2000. "Il disegno della superficie ventrale delle pinne pettorali dei Selaci come carattere diagnostico per il riconoscimento delle specie." *Annales, Series historia naturalis*, 10(2): 187–198.

_____. 2001. *Squali delle acque italiane. Guida sintetica al riconoscimento*. Ireco, Formello, 72 pp.

_____. 2002. *Lo squalo bianco nei mari d'Italia*. Ireco, Formello, 144 pp.

De Maddalena, A., and H. Baensch. 2005. *Haie im Mittelmeer*. Franckh-Kosmos Verlags-GmbH & Co., Stuttgart, 240 pp.

De Maddalena, A., O. Glaizot, and G. Oliver. 2003. "On the great white shark, *Carcharodon carcharias* (Linnaeus, 1758), preserved in the Museum of Zoology in Lausanne." *Marine Life*, 13(1/2): 53–59.

De Maddalena, A., and L. Piscitelli. 2001. "Analisi preliminare dei selaci registrati presso il mercato ittico di Milano" (aprile–settembre 2000). *Bollettino del Museo civico di Storia naturale di Venezia*, 52: 129–145.

De Maddalena, A., A. Preti, and R. Smith. 2005. *Mako sharks*. Krieger Publishing, Malabar, 72 pp.

De Maddalena, A., M. Zuffa, L. Lipej L., and A. Celona. 2001. "An analysis of the photographic evidences of the largest great white sharks, *Carcharodon carcharias* (Linnaeus, 1758), captured in the Mediterranean Sea with considerations about the maximum size of the species." *Annales, Series historia naturalis*, 11(2): 193–206.

Dunbrack, R., and R. Zielinski. 2003. "Seasonal and diurnal activity of sixgill sharks (*Hexanchus griseus*) on a shallow water reef in the Strait of Georgia, British Columbia." *Canadian Journal of Zoology*, 81(6): 1107–1111.

Ebert, D.A. 1994. "Diet of the sixgill shark *Hexanchus griseus* off southern Africa." *South African Journal of Marine Science*, 14: 213–218.

_____. 2003. *Sharks, rays and chimaeras of California*. University of California Press, Berkeley and Los Angeles, 286 pp.

Ebert, D.A., L.J.V. Compagno, and P.D. Cowley. 1992. "A preliminary investigation of the feeding ecology of squaloid sharks off the west coast of southern Africa." *South African Journal of Marine Science*, 12: 601–609.

Ellis, R. 1983. *The book of sharks*. Robert Hale, London, 256 pp.

Ellis, R., and J.E. McCosker. 1991. *Great white shark*. Stanford University Press, Stanford, 270 pp.

Francis, M.P. 1996. "Observations on a pregnant white shark with a review of reproductive biology." Pp. 157–172 in Klimley, A.P., and D.G. Ainley (eds.), *Great white sharks: The biology of* Carcharodon carcharias. Academic Press, San Diego, 518 pp.

Francis, M.P., and K.P. Mulligan. 1998. "Age and growth of New Zealand school shark, *Galeorhinus galeus*." *New Zealand Journal of Marine and Freshwater Research*, 32(3): 427–440.

Froese, R., and D. Pauly (eds). 2006. *FishBase*. World Wide Web electronic publication. www.fishbase.org, version (02/2006).

Garrick, J.A.F. 1967. "Revision of sharks of genus *Isurus* with description of a new species (Galeoidea, Lamnidae)." *Proceedings of the United States National Museum*, 118: 663–690.

_____. 1982. "Sharks of the genus *Carcharhinus*." *NOAA Technical Report NMFS Circular*, 445: 1–194.

Goldman, K.J., S.D. Anderson, J.E. McCosker, and A.P. Klimley. 1996. "Temperature, swimming depth, and movements of a white shark at the South Farallon Islands, California." Pp. 111–120 in Klimley, A.P., and D.G. Ainley (eds.), *Great white sharks: The biology of* Carcharodon carcharias. Academic Press, San Diego, 518 pp.

Hannan, K. 2005. "Determination of gastric evacuation rate for spiny dogfish, *Squalus acanthias*." *First International Symposium on the Management & Biology of Dogfish Sharks. June 13–15, 2005, Seattle, Washington. Abstracts*: 9.

Hanson, D.L. 1999. "Management of shark fisheries off the west coast of the USA." Pp. 656–681 in Shotton, R. (ed.), *Case studies of the management of elasmobranch fisheries*. FAO Fisheries Technical Paper. No. 378, part 2. FAO, Rome, pp. 480–920.

Hart, J. 1973. "Pacific fishes of Canada." *Fisheries Research Board of Canada Bulletin*, 180: 1–740.

Hemida, F., and N. Labidi. 2001. "Estimation de la croissance par analyse des fréquences de taille du requin-ha." *Rapport du 36ème Congrès de la CIESM*, Monte-Carlo, 274 pp.

Hulbert, L.B., M.F. Sigler, and C.R. Lunsford. 2006. "Depth and movement behaviour of the Pacific sleeper shark in the north-east Pacific Ocean." *Journal of Fish Biology*, 69(2): 406–425.

Jardas, I. 1972. "Supplement to the knowledge of ecology of some adriatic cartilaginous fishes (Chondrichthyes) with special reference to their nutrition." *Acta Adriatica*, 14(7): 1–60.

Johnson, R.H. 1978. *Sharks of Polynesia*. Les Editions du Pacifique, Papeete, 170 pp.

Jones, B.C., and G.H. Geen. 1977. "Observations on the brown catshark, *Apristurus brunneus* (Gilbert), in British Columbia waters." *Syesis*, 10: 169–170.

Jones, T.S., and K.I. Ugland. 2001. "Reproduction of female spiny dogfish, *Squalus acanthias*, in the Oslofjord." *Fishery Bulletin*, 99: 685–690.

Kabasakal, H. 2001. "Preliminary data on the feeding ecology of some selachians from the north-eastern Aegean Sea." *Acta Adriatica*, 42(2): 15–24.

_____. 2002. "Cephalopods in the stomach contents of four Elasmobranch species from the northern Aegean Sea." *Acta Adriatica*, 43(1): 17–24.

Klimley, A.P., B.J. Le Boeuf, K.M. Cantara, J.E. Richert, S.F. Davis, S. Van Sommeran, and J.T. Kelly. 2001. "The hunting strategy of white sharks (*Carcharodon carcharias*) near a seal colony." *Marine Biology*, 138: 617–636.

Klimley, A.P., P. Pyle, and S.D. Anderson. 1996. "Tail slap and breach: agonistic displays among white sharks?" Pp. 241–255 in Klimley, A.P. and D.G. Ainley (eds.), *Great white sharks: The biology of* Carcharodon carcharias. Academic Press, San Diego, 518 pp.

Kohler, N.E., J.G. Casey, and P.A. Turner. 1996. "Length-length and length-weight relationships for 13 shark species from the Western North Atlantic." *NOAA Technical Memorandum NMFS-NE-110*: 1–22.

Last, P.R., and J.D. Stevens. 1994. *Sharks and rays of Australia*. CSIRO, Australia, 514 pp.

Le Boeuf, B. 2004. "Hunting and migratory movements of white sharks in the eastern North Pacific." *Mem. Natl. Inst. Polar Res.*, Spec. Issue, 58: 91–102.

Le Brasseur, R.J. 1964. "Stomach Contents of Blue Shark Taken in the Gulf of Alaska." *Journal Fisheries Research Board of Canada*, 21(4): 861–862.

Lineaweaver, T.H. III, and R.H. Backus. 1969. *The Natural History of sharks*. J.B. Lippincott Co., Philadelphia, 256 pp.

Lipej, L., A. De Maddalena, and A. Soldo. 2004. *Sharks of the Adriatic Sea*. Knjiznica Annales Majora, Koper, 254 pp.

Litvinov, F.F., and V.V. Laptikhovsky. 2005. "Methods of investigations of shark heterodonty and dental formulae's variability with the blue shark, *Prionace glauca* taken as an example." *ICES CM DOCUMENTS 2005*, Theme Session on Elasmobranch Fisheries Science (N):27, International Council for the Exploration of the Sea.

Lo Bianco, S. 1909. "Notizie biologiche riguardanti specialmente il periodo di maturità sessuale degli animali del Golfo di Napoli." *Mittheilungen aus der Zoologischen Station zu Neapel*, 19(4): 513–761.

Long, D.J., and R.E. Jones. 1996. "White Shark predation and scavenging on Cetaceans in the Eastern North Pacific Ocean." Pp. 293–307 in Klimley, A.P., and D.G. Ainley (eds.), *Great white sharks: The biology of* Carcharodon carcharias. Academic Press, San Diego, 518 pp.

Lucifora, L.O., R.C. Menni, and A.H. Escalante. 2003. "Reproduction of the shark *Galeorhinus galeus* from Argentina: support for a single Southwestern Atlantic population." *AES Abstracts Manaus, Brazil, June 27–June 30*: 22.

Martin, R.A. 1995. *Shark smart: the divers' guide to understanding shark behaviour*. Diving Naturalist Press, Vancouver, 180 pp.

_____. 2003. *Field Guide to the Great White Shark*. ReefQuest Centre for Shark Research, Special Publication No. 1, 192 pp.

_____. 2004. "Northerly distribution of white sharks (*Carcharodon carcharias*) in the eastern Pacific and its Relation to ENSO Events." *Marine Fisheries Review*, 66(1): 16–26.

Matthews, L.H. 1962. "The shark that hibernates." *New Scientist*, 280: 415–421.

McCosker, J.E. 1987. "The white shark, *Carcharodon carcharias*, has a warm stomach." *Copeia*, 1987: 195–197.

McFarlane, G.A., and J.R. King. 2003. "Migrations patterns of spiny dogfish (*Squalus acanthias*) in the North Pacific Ocean." *Fishery Bulletin*, 101: 358–367.

Michael, S.W. 1993. *Reef sharks and rays of the world.* Sea Challengers, Monterey, 107 pp.

Miller, D.J., and R.S. Collier. 1981. "Shark attacks in California and Oregon, 1926–1979." *California Fish & Game*, 67(2): 76–104.

Mollet, H.F., and G.M. Cailliet. 1996. "Using allometry to predict body mass from linear measurements of the white shark." Pp. 81–90 in Klimley, A.P., and D.G. Ainley (eds.), *Great white sharks. The biology of* Carcharodon carcharias. Academic Press, San Diego, 518 pp.

Mollet, H.F., G.M. Cailliet, A.P. Klimley, D.A. Ebert, A.D. Testi and L.J.V. Compagno. 1996. "A review of length validation methods and protocols to measure large white sharks." Pp. 91–108 in Klimley, A.P., and D.G. Ainley (eds.), *Great white sharks. The biology of* Carcharodon carcharias. Academic Press, San Diego, 518 pp.

Mollet, H.F., G. Cliff, H.L. Pratt Jr., and J.D. Stevens. 2000. "Reproductive biology of the female shortfin mako, *Isurus oxyrinchus* Rafinesque, 1810, with comments on the embryonic development of lamnoids." *Fishery Bulletin*, 98: 299–318.

Moreno, J.A. 1989. "Biología reproductiva y fenología de *Alopias vulpinus* (Bonnaterre, 1788) en el Atlántico Nororiental y Mediterráneo Occidental." *Scientia Marina*, 1989, 53(1): 37–46.

_____. 1995. *Guía de los tiburones del Atlántico Nororiental y Mediterráneo.* Ed. Pirámide, Madrid, 310 pp.

Mueter, F.J., and B.L. Norcross. 2002. "Spatial and temporal patterns in the demersal fish community on the shelf on upper slope regions of the Gulf of Alaska." *Fisheries Bulletin*, 100(3): 559–581.

Muñoz-Chapuli, R. 1984. "Ethologie de la reproduction chez qualques requins de l'Atlantique Nord-Est." *Cybium*, 8(3): 1–14.

Myrberg, A. Jr. 1987. "Shark behaviour." Pp. 84–92 in Stevens, J.D. (ed.), *Sharks*. Intercontinental Publishing Corporation Limited, Hong Kong, 240 pp.

Nagasawa, K. 1998. "Predation by salmon sharks (*Lamna ditropis*) on Pacific salmon (*Oncorhynchus spp.*) in the North Pacific Ocean." *North Pacific Anadromous Fish Commission*, 2: 419–433.

Nagasawa, K., T. Azumaya, and Y. Ishida. 2002. "Impact of Predation by Salmon Sharks (*Lamna ditropis*) and Daggertooth (*Anotopterus nikparini*) on Pacific Salmon (*Oncorhynchus spp.*) Stocks in the North Pacific Ocean." *NPAFC Technical Report*, 4: 51–52.

Palsson, W.A. 2005. "Status of Spiny Dogfish in Puget Sound, Washington." *First International Symposium on the Management & Biology of Dogfish Sharks. June 13–15, 2005, Seattle, Washington. Abstracts*: 21.

Parker, H.W., and M. Boeseman. 1954. "The basking shark, *Cetorhinus maximus*, in winter." *Proceedings of the Zoological Society of London*, 124(1): 185–194.

Patokina, F.A., and F.F. Litvinov. 2004. "Food composition and distribution of demersal elasmobranches on shelf and upper slope of North-West Africa." *International Council for the Exploration of the Sea, CM 2004/K:19*.

Paust, B.C., and R. Smith. 1986. "Salmon shark manual: The development of a commercial salmon shark, *Lamna ditropis*, fishery in the North Pacific." *Alaska Sea Grant Report*, 86-01: 1– 430.

Poll, M. 1951. "Poissons. 1. Generalités. 2. Sélaciens et Chimères." *Result. Sci. Exped. Oceanogr. Belge*, 4(1): 1–154.

Pratt, H.L. Jr. 1996. "Reproduction in the male white shark." Pp. 131–138 in Klimley, A.P. and D.G. Ainley (eds.), *Great white sharks. The biology of* Carcharodon carcharias. Academic Press, San Diego, 518 pp.

Preti, A., S.E. Smith, and D.A. Ramon. 2001. "Feeding habits of the common thresher shark (*Alopias vulpinus*) sampled from the California-based drift gill net fishery, 1998–99." *California Cooperative Oceanic Fisheries Investigations Reports*, 42: 145–152.

Randall, J.E. 1986. *Sharks of Arabia*. IMMEL Publishing, London, 148 pp.

Ranzi, S. 1932-1934. "Le basi fisio-morfologiche dello sviluppo embrionale dei Selaci. 1, 2, 3." *Pubbl. Stazione Zoologica di Napoli*, 12–13.

Ribot Carballal, C., R. Felix Uraga, and F. Galvan Magaña. 2003. "Age and growth of the shortfin mako, *Isurus oxyrinchus*, from Baja California Sur, Mexico." *AES Abstracts Manaus, Brazil, June 27–June 30*: 6.

Roedel, P.M., and W.E. Ripley. 1950. "California sharks and rays." *Fishery Bulletin*, (75): 1–88.

Sciarrotta, T.C., and D.R. Nelson. 1977. "Diel behavior of the blue shark, *Prionace glauca*, near Santa Catalina Island, California." *Fishery Bulletin*, 75(3): 519–528.

Shestopal, I.P., O.V. Smirnov, and A.A. Grekov. 2002. "Bottom long-line fishing for deepwater sharks on sea-mounts in the International waters of the North Atlantic." *NAFO SCR Doc. 02/100*, Ser. No. N4721, 5 pp.

Siccardi, E.M. 1971. "*Cetorhinus* in el Atlantico sur (Elasmobranchii: Cetorhinidae)." *Revista del Museo Argentino de Ciencias Naturales "Bernardino Rivadavia,"* 6(2): 61–101.

Sigler, M.F., L.B. Hulbert, C.R. Lunsford, N.H. Thompson, K. Burek, G. O'Corry-Crowe, and A.C. Hirons. 2006. "Diet of Pacific sleeper shark, a potential Steller sea lion predator, in the north-east Pacific Ocean." *Journal of Fish Biology*, 69(2): 392–405.

Sims, D.W., and V.A. Quayle. 1998. "Selective foraging behaviour of basking sharks on zooplankton in a small-scale front." *Nature*, 393: 460–464.

Skomal, G.B., and L.J. Natanson. 2002. "Age and growth of the blue shark, *Prionace glauca*, in the North Atlantic Ocean." *Col. Vol. Sci. Pap. ICCAT*, 54(4): 1212–1230.

Smale, M.J., and P.C. Heemstra. 1997. "First record of albinism in the great white shark, *Carcharodon carcharias* (Linnaeus, 1758)." *South African Journal of Science*, 93: 243–245.

Soldat, V.T. 2002. "Spiny dogfish (*Squalus acanthias* L.) of the Northwest Atlantic Ocean (NWA)." *Northwest Atlantic Fisheries Organization, Scientific Council Meeting* – September 2002: 1–33.

Stevens, J.D. (ed.). 1987. *Sharks*. Intercontinental Publishing Corporation Limited, Hong Kong, 240 pp.

Stillwell, C. 1991. "The ravenous mako." Pp. 77–88 in Gruber, S.H. (ed.), "Discovering sharks." *Underwater Naturalist, Bulletin American Littoral Society*, 19(4)–20(1).

Strong, W.R. Jr. 1996. "Shape discrimination and visual predatory tactics in white sharks." Pp. 229–240 in Klimley, A.P., and D.G. Ainley (eds.), *Great white sharks. The biology of* Carcharodon carcharias. Academic Press, San Diego, 518 pp.

Tortonese, E. 1956. *Fauna d'Italia vol. II. Leptocardia, Ciclostomata, Selachii.* Calderini, Bologna, 334 pp.

_____. 1985. "Gli squali Mediterranei del genere *Hexanchus* (Chondrichthyes)." *Atti della Societa Italiana di Scienze Naturali e Museo Civico di Storia Naturale di Milano*, 126 (3-4): 137–140.

Tribuzio, C., and G.H. Kruse. 2005. "Report of an ongoing investigation of the life history, ecology and population dynamics of spiny dogfish, *Squalus acanthias*, in Alaska." *First International Symposium on the Management & Biology of Dogfish Sharks. June 13–15, 2005, Seattle, Washington. Abstracts*: 15.

Tricas, T.C., and J.E. McCosker. 1984. "Predatory behavior of the white shark (*Carcharodon carcharias*) with notes on its biology." *Proceedings of the California Academy of Sciences*, 43(14): 221–238.

Uchida, S., M. Toda, K. Teshima, and K. Yano. 1996. "Pregnant white sharks and full-term embryos from Japan." Pp. 139–155 in Klimley, A.P., and D.G. Ainley (eds.), *Great white sharks: The biology of* Carcharodon carcharias. Academic Press, San Diego, 518 pp.

Van Deinse, A.B., and M.J. Adriani. 1953. "On the absence of gill rakers in specimens of the basking shark, *Cetorhinus maximus* (Gunner)." *Zoologische Mededelingen*, 31(27): 307–310.

Vannuccini, S. 1999. "Shark utilization, marketing and trade." *FAO Fisheries Technical Paper*, 389: 1–470.

Walker, T. 1999. "*Galeorhinus galeus* fisheries of the world." Pp. 728–773 in Shotton, R. (ed.), *Case studies of the management of elasmobranch fisheries.* FAO Fisheries Technical Paper. No. 378, part 2. FAO, Rome, pp. 480–920.

Wallace, S., and B. Gisborne. 2006. *Basking Sharks. The Slaughter of BC's Gentle Giants.* New Star Books, Vancouver, 96 pp.

Watts, S. 2001. *The end of the line?* WildAid, San Francisco, 62 pp.

Weng, K.C., P.C. Castilho, J.M. Morrissette, A. Landeira, R.J. Schallert, D.B. Holts, K.J. Goldman, and B.A. Block. 2005. "Satellite Tagging and Cardiac Physiology Reveal Niche Expansion in Salmon Sharks." *Science*, 310:104–106.

White, W.T., and I.C. Potter. 2004. "Habitat partitioning among four elasmobranch species in nearshore, shallow waters of a subtropical embayment in Western Australia." *Marine Biology*, 145: 1023–1032.

Whitehead, P.J.P., M.-L.Bauchot, J.C. Hureau, J. Nielsen, and E. Tortonese (eds.). 1984. *Fishes of the North-Eastern Atlantic and the Mediterranean. Vol. 1.* Unesco, Paris.

Index